Hill & Valley

LOG CABINS

Robert DeCarli

Located in Paducah, Kentucky, the American Quilter's Society (AQS) is dedicated to promoting the accomplishments of today's quilters. Through its publications and events, AQS strives to honor today's quiltmakers and their work and to inspire future creativity and innovation in quiltmaking.

Executive Book Editor: Andi Milam Reynolds
Senior Book Editor: Linda Baxter Lasco
Graphic Design: Lynda Smith
Cover Design: Michael Buckingham
Quilt Photography: Charles R. Lynch

Additional copies of this book may be ordered from the American Quilter's Society, PO Box 3290, Paducah, KY 42002-3290, or online at www.AmericanQuilter.com.

Text © 2012, Author, Robert DeCarli
Artwork © 2012, American Quilter's Society

Library of Congress Cataloging-in-Publication Data

DeCarli, Robert.
  Hill & valley log cabins / by Robert DeCarli.
    p. cm.
  Summary: "Author shows how to use rectangles to make curved log cabin blocks along with using color and value to create optical illusions. 13 projects from wallhangings to bed quilts with graphic, geometric designs for a modern look"--Provided by publisher.
  ISBN 978-1-60460-053-7
  1. Patchwork--Patterns. 2. Quilting. 3. Log cabin quilts.
I. Title.
  TT835.D42 2013
  746.46--dc23
                        2012043206

Dedication

To Kathleen, who started it all. She wasn't a quilter but wanted help in making a quilt for our daughter's wedding. I wasn't a quilter but I made a simple Four-Patch and was hooked. We made the wedding quilt and started a quilting journey that has enriched our lives beyond measure.

Acknowledgments

I am very grateful to the members of the Penn Oaks Quilt Guild who made the most astonishing set of quilts. When I found that we needed all the quilts for the book, they jumped right in and made quilts beyond my wildest expectations. I will never be able to thank them enough. They are:

Sara Beyer Borr, Downingtown, Pennsylvania

Kathleen DeCarli, Downingtown, Pennsylvania—my wife

Elaine F. Egan, Downingtown, Pennsylvania

Jean Fox, West Chester, Pennsylvania

Fay Ann Grider, Gulph Mills, Pennsylvania

Delores A. Holzwarth, Downingtown, Pennsylvania

Roberta Lodi, Downingtown, Pennsylvania

Robin McMillen, Downingtown, Pennsylvania—my daughter

Ellen J. McMillen, Downingtown, Pennsylvania—the mother-in-law

Kelly P. Meanix, Downingtown, Pennsylvania

Myrna M. Paluba, Wayne, Pennsylvania

Patricia A. Sherman, Lancaster, Pennsylvania

Patricia A. Smith, Downingtown, Pennsylvania

Cynthia Vognetz, Phoenixville, Pennsylvania

Photo by Robert DeCarli
Standing (left to right): Ellen McMillen, Robin McMillen, Kathy DeCarli, Jean Fox, Pat Smith, Myrna Paluba, Fay Ann Grider, Rob Lodi; Seated (left to right): Sara Borr, Kelly Meanix, Cindy Vognetz, Delores Holzwarth, Elaine Egan, Pat Sherman

Special thanks to Carol Lee Heisler of Lorac Designs, East Norriton, Pennsylvania, for the quilting of many of these quilts. www.loracdesignsclh.com.

Contents

DIAMOND STAR II, 68" x 68", pieced by Pat Sherman, Lancaster, Pennsylvania, and quilted by Kim Loar, Lancaster, Pennsylvania

Pat used the same setting as DIAMOND STAR (page 40) but with the V8-V4 block instead of the V8-H4-V2 block. Taking out the H4 portion of the block eliminates the small circular and semi-circular pattern but highlights the diamond shapes.

Introduction: Serendipity Strikes Again

It all started while waiting for my "better half" in the incredible heat at the Vermont Quilt Festival. My class let out early and after doing some shopping, I went to the classrooms to wait for "she said." I bought *Ghost Layers & Color Washes* by Katie Pasquini Masopust for no other reason than that her stuff is just fabulous.

I am not an appliquér and I don't do colors really well as I am color blind. Still, Katie's work is just too incredible to not look at. So, I sat there looking at the book, trying to figure out how to apply her ghosts and color washes techniques to the piecing world. The basic idea behind the "ghosts" is to find shadows or similar structures in the quilt and then superimpose them on the quilt. You then "paint" parts of the quilt with colors different from those used in the quilt.

I needed something that had obvious shadows or ghosts and that I could easily paint, while still being able to piece. I immediately thought of the Log Cabin block.

Figure 1. Log Cabin block

The square and triangle shapes would be the shadows (ghosts) and the painting could be done along the log lines or on the diagonals. The next question was size—small, medium, or big blocks? Since I never go anywhere without graph paper, I pulled the emergency piece from my wallet and drew a 2", 4", and 8" square to see the relative sizes (Figure 2).

I immediately dismissed the 2" block as being too small to work with. The 8" was a possibility, but you need many shadows and a variety of paint and I thought it would just be too big and complex. That left the 4" block. I decided that 8 by 8 (64 blocks) would be big enough, so I made a note and went back to sitting and waiting.

I kept glancing at the graph paper as something seemed odd. The 2-in-4, the 4-in-8—I began to wonder if the 2" would fit in the 4" along straight sewing lines. That is, if we carved out a 2" square from the 4" (and a 4" square from the 8"), would what's left (the dotted sections in Figure 2) be along seam lines and easy to sew or would it just be so complicated that it wouldn't be worth doing? I made another note and went back to waiting.

Figure 2. 2-in-4-in-8

I started the GHOST quilt using 4" Curved Log Cabin blocks the day we returned from Vermont.

GHOST, 40" x 40", pieced and quilted by the author

But the 2-in-4 and the 4-in-8 kept rattling around in my head. I finally cranked up my EQ5 software to see if there was anything to this. To my wondrous surprise, it turned out perfectly! The 2" square fit nicely in the 4", leaving straight line rectangular sections to construct. The 4" square fit just as nicely in the 8".

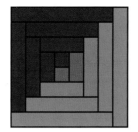

Figure 3. Basic 8" Log Cabin block

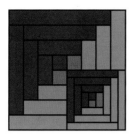

Figure 4. 8" block with a 4" Log Cabin block inserted in the lower right-hand corner

Figure 5. Small Barn Raising set using the standard 8" Log Cabin block

Figure 6. The same set using a 4" Log Cabin block fit into an 8" Log Cabin block.

Figure 3 shows the basic 8" log block. Figure 4 shows the 8" block with a 4" log block inserted in the lower right hand corner. Figure 5 shows a small Barn Raising quilt using the standard 8" Log Cabin block. Figure 6 shows the same quilt, using a 4" log block fit into an 8" log block. The possibilities and variations are endless.

It turned out that the 2" block fit in the 4" block, and in the same way, the 4" block fit in the 8" block, leaving rectangular log-like pieces to construct, all along the seam lines of the original block. But, it was even better than this. You get a curved effect if you vary the widths of the logs.

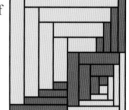

Figure 7. 8" Curved Log Cabin block with a 4" Curved Log Cabin block insert

Figure 8. Barn Raising set using the Curved Log Cabin block

The 2-in-4-in-8 works equally well with these blocks. This gives a whole new set of blocks that can be used to make variations of traditional Log Cabin quilts.

Hill & Valley Log Cabin Blocks

Overview

The 8" Curved Log Cabin block is the foundation for all the Hill & Valley blocks.

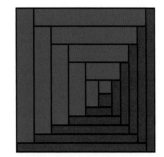

Figure 1. 8" Curved Log Cabin block

We can insert a 4" Curved Log Cabin block in the lower right-hand corner. This gives one set of blocks.

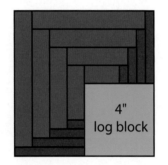

Figure 2. 8" block with 4" insert

In addition, you can insert a 2" Curved Log Cabin block in the lower right-hand corner of the 4" block. This gives another set of blocks.

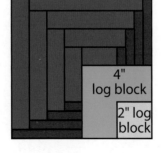

Figure 3. 8" block with 4" insert with a 2" insert

The Valley8 (V8) Block

To see why and how this works, you have to look at the construction of the 8" Curved Log Cabin block (V8).

Start with a ¾" (finished) red square (Figure 4). Working in a counter-clockwise direction, add a ¾" blue square, followed

by a ¾" x 1½" blue log. From this point on, the blue logs are 1" wide (finished) and all the red logs are ½" wide (finished). The lengths of the logs (specified in the projects) have no impact on the piecing.

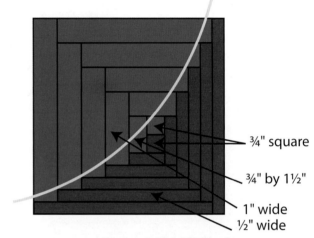

Figure 4. The V8 block

The block configuration given in Figure 4 is the basis for all the blocks. The "curve" runs from bottom left to upper right, creating a partial "valley." We call this the Valley8 block—V8 for short. Other configurations are dealt with in Variations on a Theme (pages 76–78).

If you count up from the bottom right corner, you will see that the 4" mark falls right on a seam line in the center (Figure 5).

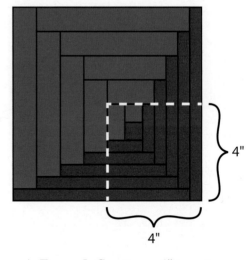

Figure 5. Creating a 4" insert

You can now break the block into three sections (Figure 6).

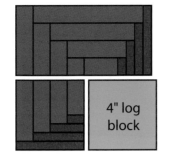

Figure 6. Constructing the block in 3 sections

The top and bottom left sections are "log-like" and easily pieced. The bottom right section is simply a 4" Curved Log Cabin block. You can use two configurations for the 4" block. The first configuration is the same as the V8 block (Figure 7), with the curve going from bottom left to upper right, forming a valley. This is called the V4 block. If you turn the block two times clockwise (Figure 8), you get the second configuration. The curve forms a hill and we name this the H4 block.

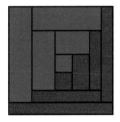
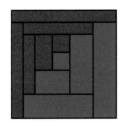

Figure 7. The V4 block   *Figure 8. The H4 block*

The V4 in the V8 or the H4 in the V8 give us another set of blocks.

The Valley4 (V4) Block

The 4" block can be divided into sections in the exact same way as the 8" block. You can carve out a 2" square from the 4" block along the seam lines, leaving two log-like sections that are easily pieced. Start with a ½" (finished) blue square sort of in the center. From this point on, all the red logs are ½" wide (finished) and all the blue logs are 1" wide (finished). The lengths of the logs (specified in the projects) have no impact on the piecing.

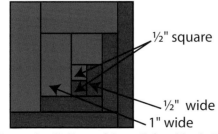

Figure 9. 4" Curved Log Cabin block (V4)

If you count up from the bottom-right corner, you will see that the 2" mark falls right on a seam line in the center (Figure 10). You can now break the block into three sections.

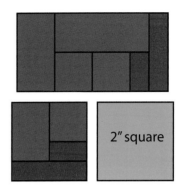

Figure 10. V4 block divided into 3 sections

The top and bottom left sections are "log-like" and easily pieced. The bottom right section is a 2" Curved Log Cabin block. You can use two configurations for the 2" block. The first is the same as the V8 block with the curve going from bottom left to upper right, forming a valley. This is called the V2 block. If you turn the block two times clockwise, you get the second configuration where the curve is hill-like. We name this the H2 block.

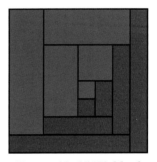

Figure 11. 2" V2 block

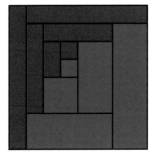

Figure 12. 2" H2 block

The Hill & Valley blocks are constructed exactly the same. It is simply the orientation of the blocks that makes the difference.

The Hill4 (H4) Block

If we look at the construction of the Hill4 (4" Curved Log Cabin) block (Figure 13), we see that the same thing happens.

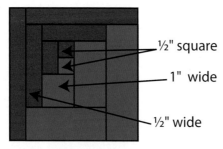

½" square

1" wide

½" wide

Figure 13. Hill4 (H4) 4" Curved Log Cabin block

You can carve out a 2" square along the seam lines, leaving two log-like sections that are easily pieced. Start with a ½" (finished) blue square. As with the V4 block, from this point on, all the red logs are ½" wide (finished) and all the blue logs are 1" wide (finished). The lengths of the logs (specified in the projects) have no impact on the piecing.

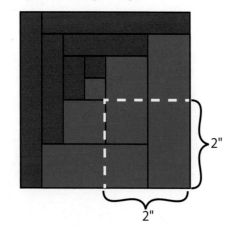

2"

2"

Figure 14. Carving out a 2" block

If you count up from the bottom-right corner, you will see that the 2" mark falls right on a seam line in the center (Figure 14). You can now break the block into 3 sections (Figure 15).

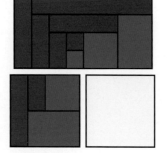

Figure 15. The H4 block divided into 3 sections

The top- and bottom-left sections are log-like and easily pieced. The bottom-right section is a 2" Log Cabin block. You can use either the V2 or H2 for the 2" block.

The various combinations of the 2-in-4-in-8 give us yet another set of blocks.

The Blocks

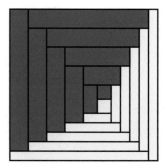

Valley8 (V8): 8" Curved Log Cabin block

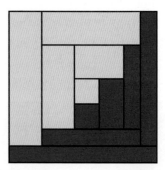

Valley4 (V4): 4" Curved Log Cabin block

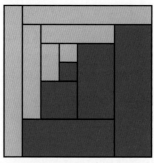

Hill4 (H4): 4" Curved Log Cabin block (the V4 block turned twice clockwise)

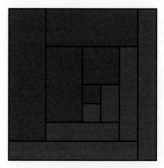

Valley2 (V2): 2" Curved Log Cabin block

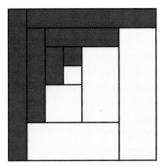

Hill2 (H2): 2" Curved Log Cabin block (the V2 block turned twice clockwise)

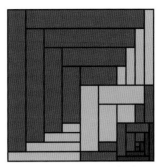

Valley8-Valley4-Valley2 (V8-V4-V2): 8" Curved Log Cabin block with a 4" Curved Log Cabin block insert with a 2" Curved Log Cabin block insert

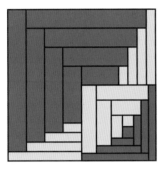

Valley8-Valley4 (V8-V4): 8" Curved Log Cabin block with a 4" Curved Log Cabin block insert

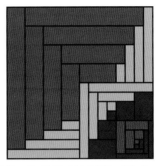

Valley8-Hill4-Valley2 (V8-H4-V2): 8" Curved Log Cabin block with a twice-turned 4" Curved Log Cabin block insert with a 2" Curved Log Cabin block insert

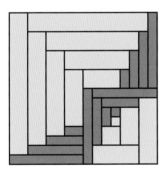

Valley8-Hill4 (V8-H4): 8" Curved Log Cabin block with a twice-turned 4" Curved Log Cabin block insert

Valley8-Hill4-Hill2 (V8-H4-H2): 8" Curved Log Cabin block with a twice-turned 4" Curved Log Cabin block insert with a 2" twice-turned Curved Log Cabin block insert

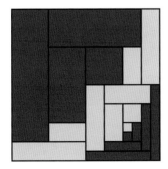

Valley4-Valley2 (V4-V2): 4" Curved Log Cabin block with a 2" Curved Log Cabin block insert

Piecing the Blocks

All the block variations are pieced in the same way as the Valley8 block. All can be pieced in two different ways:

Chain piecing

Traditional piecing

Piecing the Valley8 (V8) Block

The V8 block is constructed from the inside out. Start with the center piece and work in a counterclockwise direction, adding light strips to two adjacent sides and dark strips to the other two sides. The strip sizes are given with each project. The piecing sequence and finished V8 block are shown below.

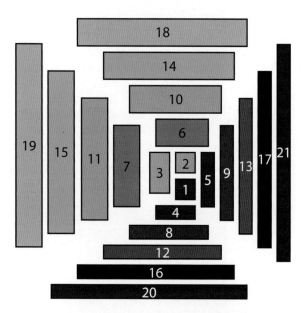

Figure 1. V8 block piecing sequence

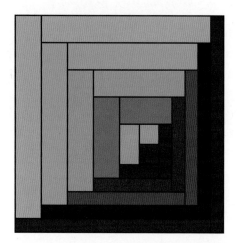

Figure 2. The completed V8 block

To chain piece this block, sew a strip of fabric 1 to a strip of fabric 2. From this, cut the 1-2 sections. Square up, turn on end, and sew to a fabric 3 strip. From this, cut the 1-2-3 sections. Square up, turn on end, and sew to a fabric 4 strip. From this, you cut the 1-2-3-4 sections.

Continue in the same manner for the remaining strips. You can chain piece all the blocks and all the sections of the blocks.

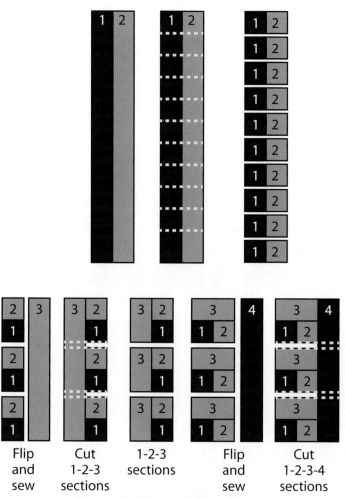

Figure 3. Chain piecing sequence

The Valley4 (V4), Valley2 (V2), Hill4 (H4), and Hill2 (H2) Blocks

The structure of the V4 and V2 blocks is identical. The difference is that the V4 block uses 1" and ½" (finished) strips while the V2 block uses ½" and ¼" (finished) strips.

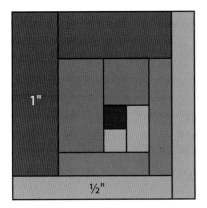
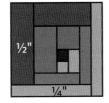

Figure 4. The V4 block   *Figure 5. The V2 block*

The V4 and V2 blocks are constructed in the same way—from the inside out.

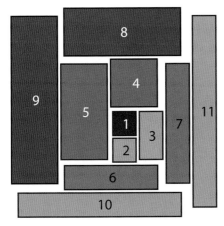

Figure 6. Piecing sequence for the V4 and V2 blocks

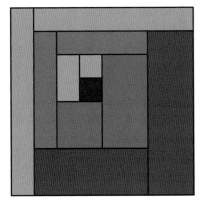
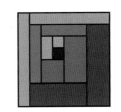

Figure 7. Turn the V4 block two times clockwise to get the H4 block.

Figure 8. Turn the V2 block two times clockwise to get the H2 block.

The Valley8-Valley4 (V8-V4) Block

The V8-V4 block is built off the V8 block by inserting a V4 block in the lower right-hand corner.

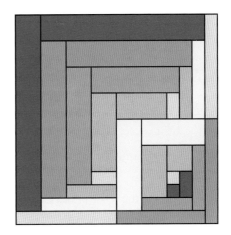

Figure 9. The V8-V4 block

This block is constructed in 3 sections.

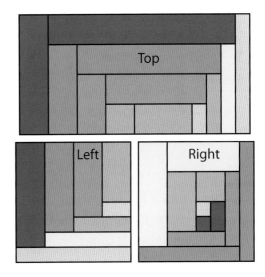

Figure 10. The V8-V4 block divided into 3 sections

The top section and the lower-left section are portions of a Curved Log Cabin block.

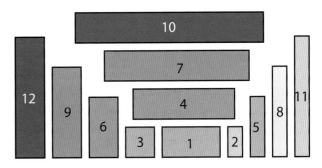

Figure 11. Piecing sequence for the top section

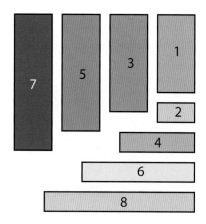

Figure 12. Piecing sequence for lower-left section

The lower right section is the V4 Curved Log Cabin block.

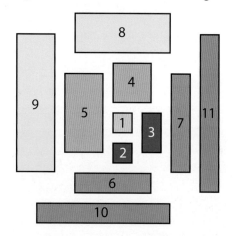

Figure 13. Piecing sequence for the V4 insert

The Valley8-Hill4 (V8-H4) Block

The V8-H4 block is built off the V8 block by inserting an H4 block in the lower right-hand corner. Remember, the H4 block is simply the V4 block turned twice clockwise.

Figure 14. The V8-H4 block

The block is constructed in 3 sections.

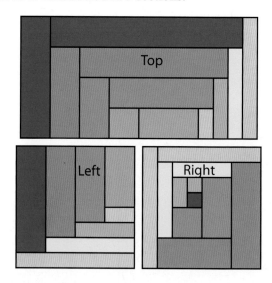

Figure 15. The V8-H4 block divided into 3 sections

The piecing sequence is shown in Figure 16. The left section is identical to the left section for the V8-V4 block and the piecing sequence is given in Figure 12. The right section is the H4 Log Cabin block, which is simply the V4 block turned twice clockwise. Note that although the piecing sequence is the same as the V4 block (Figure 13), the placement of the colors is reversed.

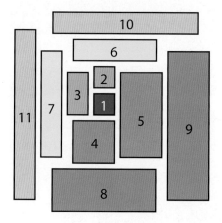

Figure 16. Piecing sequence for the lower-right H4 insert

Sew each of the sections; join the left and right sections, then add to the top section to complete the block.

The Valley4-Valley2 (V4-V2) Block

The V4-V2 block is built off the V4 block by inserting a V2 block in the lower right-hand corner.

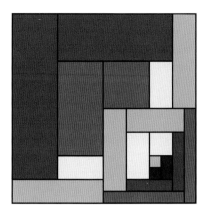

Figure 17. The V4-V2 block

The block is constructed in 3 sections.

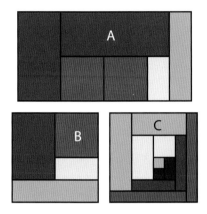

Figure 18. The V4-V2 block divided into 3 sections

The piecing sequence for each section is shown below.

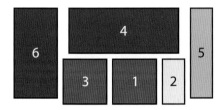

Figure 19. Piecing sequence for the top section

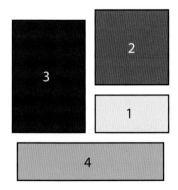

Figure 20. Piecing sequence for lower left section

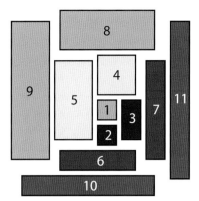

Figure 21. Piecing sequence for bottom-right section of the V2 block

Sew each of the sections; join the left and right sections, then add to the top section to complete the block.

The Valley8-Valley4-Valley2 (V8-V4-V2) Block

The V8-V4-V2 block is built off the V8 block by inserting a V4-V2 block in the lower right-hand corner.

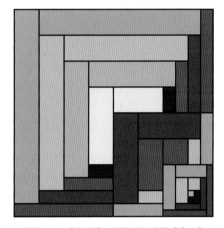

Figure 22. The V8-V4-V2 block

The block is constructed in 5 sections.

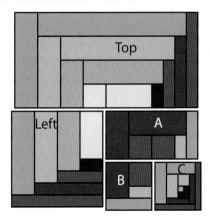

Figure 23. The V8-V4-V2 block divided into 5 sections

Piecing the Blocks

The top and left sections are pieced just like the same sections of the V8-V4 block (Figures 11 & 12, pages 11–12). Sections A, B, and C are pieced the same as the V4-V2 block (See Figures 19, 20 & 21, page 13).

Sew each of the sections; join Sections B & C, then add to Section A. Sew this unit to the left section and then add the top section to complete the block.

The Valley8-Hill4-Valley2 (V8-H4-V2) and Valley8-Hill4-Hill2 (V8-H4-H2) Blocks

The V8-H4-V2 block is built off the V8 block by inserting a H4-V2 block in the lower right-hand corner.

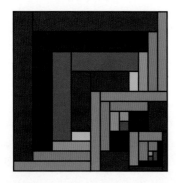

Figure 24. The V8-H4-V2 block

The block is constructed in 5 sections.

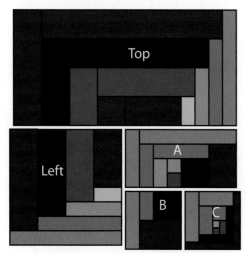

Figure 25. The V8-H4-V2 block divided into 5 sections

The top and left sections are pieced just like the same sections of the V8-V4 block (Figures 11 & 12, pages 11–12). Section A is part of the H4 Curved Log Cabin block and is built in the same way.

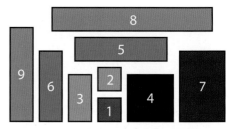

Figure 26. Piecing sequence for Section A

Section B is part of the H4 Log Cabin block and is built in the same way.

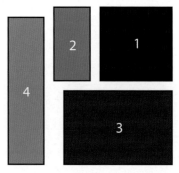

Figure 27. Piecing sequence for Section B

Section C is a Valley2 (V2) block (Figure 6, page 11).

Note: For the V8-H4-H2 block, turn section C (the V2 block) twice clockwise.

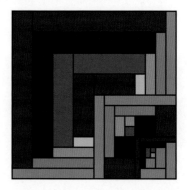

Figure 28. The V8-H4-H2 block

Sew each of the sections; join Sections B & C, then add to Section A. Sew this unit to the left section and then add the top section to complete the block.

Finishing

Each of the quilts was quilted and bound according to the favorite methods of the individual quilters. Refer to any one of the many books on finishing or pick your favorite techniques for quilting and binding your quilt.

ISLANDS IN THE STREAM II, 52" x 68", pieced and quilted by Elaine Egan, Downingtown, Pennsylvania. The softer effect of this variation of the original (page 36) is created by using the V8-V4 block in the same Barn Raising set.

ALMOST AMISH

ALMOST AMISH, 38" x 38", original design by the author, pieced and quilted by Ellen McMillen, Downingtown, Pennsylvania

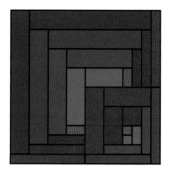

The V8-V4 block

Note the contrast between this and RINGED SQUARES (page 20), which uses the same block. The colors give the quilt an Amish look and the dark blues against the medium blues highlight the straight versus the curved lines.

Materials

Blue-1: ¼ yard	Pink-1: ⅛ yard
Blue-2: ½ yard	Fuchsia-2: ⅛ yard
Dark blue-3: 1¼ yards (includes outer border & binding)	Fuchsia-3: ¼ yard
Dark blue-4: ½ yard	Fuchsia-4: ⅝ yard (includes inner border)
Backing: 2½ yards	Batting: 46" x 46"

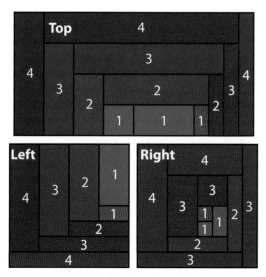

V8-V4 fabric selection

Cutting Directions

All measurements are in inches.

V8-V4					
Section	**Fabric**	**Piece**	**Width**	**Length**	**Cut**
Top	Pink-1	2	1	1½	16
	Fuchsia-2	5	1	2½	16
	Fuchsia-3	8	1	3½	16
	Fuchsia-4	11	1	4½	16
	Blue-1	1	1½	2½	16
	Blue-1	3	1½	1½	16
	Blue-2	4	1½	4	16
	Blue-2	6	1½	2½	16
	Dark blue-3	7	1½	5½	16
	Dark blue-3	9	1½	3½	16
	Dark blue-4	10	1½	7	16
	Dark blue-4	12	1½	4½	16
Left	Pink-1	1	1	1½	16
	Fuchsia-2	4	1	2½	16
	Fuchsia-3	6	1	3½	16
	Fuchsia-4	8	1	4½	16
	Blue-1	2	1½	2½	16
	Blue-2	3	1½	3	16
	Dark blue-3	5	1½	3½	16
	Dark blue-4	7	1½	4	16
Right	Pink-1	1	1	1	16
	Fuchsia-3	4	1½	1½	16
	Fuchsia-3	5	1½	2½	16
	Fuchsia-4	8	1½	3	16
	Fuchsia-4	9	1½	4	16
	Blue-1	2	1	1	16
	Blue-1	3	1	1½	16
	Blue-2	6	1	2½	16
	Blue-2	7	1	3	16
	Dark blue-3	10	1	4	16
	Dark blue-3	11	1	4½	16
Inner Border	Fuchsia-4	1½	1½	40	4
Outer Border	Dark blue-3		2½	40	4
Binding	Dark blue-3		2½	40	4

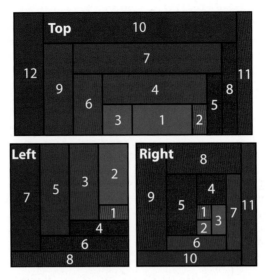

V8-V4 sewing sequence

Quilt Construction

Construct 16 blocks following the V8-V4 piecing sequence given on pages 11–12.

The blocks (B) will be oriented by turning them once (B1), twice (B2), or three times (B3).

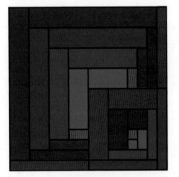 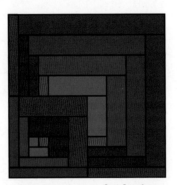 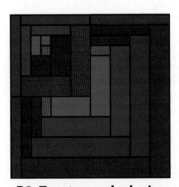 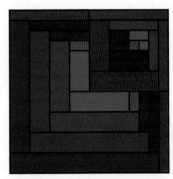

B: Block   **B1: One turn clockwise**   **B2: Two turns clockwise**   **B3: Three turns clockwise**

Block orientation

Lay out the blocks in rows according to the quilt assembly diagram. Sew the blocks into rows and sew the rows together.

For the inner border, cut 2 strips 1½" x 32½" from fuchsia-4. Sew to the sides of the quilt. Cut 2 strips 1½" x 34½" from fuchsia-4 and add to the top and bottom of the quilt.

For the outer border, cut 2 strips 2½" x 34½" from dark blue-2. Sew to the sides of the quilt. Cut 2 strips 2½" x 38½" from dark blue-2 and add to the top and bottom of the quilt.

Layer and quilt according to your favorite method. Bind and label your quilt.

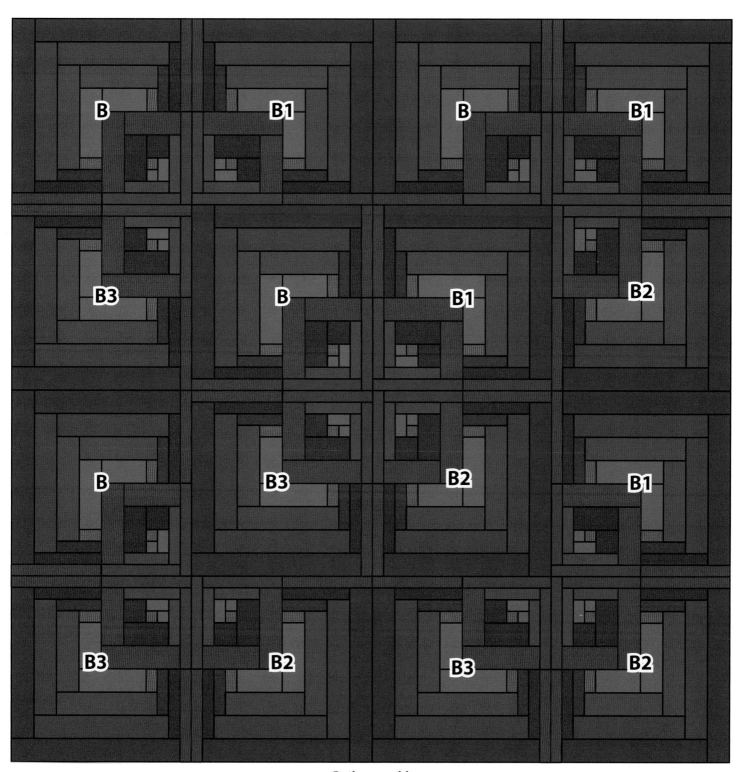

Quilt assembly

RINGED SQUARES, 68" x 68", pieced by Delores Holzwarth, Downingtown, Pennsylvania,
quilted by Carol Lee Heisler, Lorac Designs, East Norriton, Pennsylvania

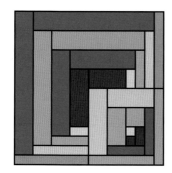

The V8-V4 block

The bold blues highlight the "square" of this setting while the golds emphasize the curve.

Materials

Blue 1: ⅞ yard	Gold 1: ¼ yard
Blue 2: 1⅛ yards	Gold 2: ⅝ yard
Blue 3: 1¼ yards	Gold 3: ⅞ yard
Blue 4: 2¼ yards (includes border and binding)	Gold 4: ½ yard
Backing: 4¼ yards	Batting: 76" x 76"

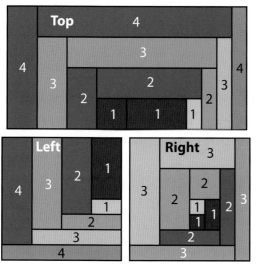

V8-V4 fabric selection

Cutting Directions

All measurements are in inches.

V8-V4					
Section	**Fabric**	**Piece**	**Width**	**Length**	**Cut**
Top	Gold-1	2	1	1½	64
	Gold-2	5	1	2½	64
	Gold-3	8	1	3½	64
	Gold-4	11	1	4½	64
	Blue-1	1	1½	2½	64
	Blue-1	3	1½	1½	64
	Blue-2	4	1½	4	64
	Blue-2	6	1½	2½	64
	Blue-3	7	1½	5½	64
	Blue-3	9	1½	3½	64
	Blue-4	10	1½	7	64
	Blue-4	12	1½	4½	64
Left	Gold-1	1	1	1½	64
	Gold-2	4	1	2½	64
	Gold-3	6	1	3½	64
	Gold-4	8	1	4½	64
	Blue-1	2	1½	2½	64
	Blue-2	3	1½	3	64
	Blue-3	5	1½	3½	64
	Blue-4	7	1½	4	64
Right	Gold-1	1	1	1	64
	Gold-2	4	1½	1½	64
	Gold-2	5	1½	2½	64
	Gold-3	8	1½	3	64
	Gold-3	9	1½	4	64
	Blue-1	2	1	1	64
	Blue-1	3	1	1½	64
	Blue-2	6	1	2½	64
	Blue-2	7	1	3	64
	Blue-3	10	1	4	64
	Blue-3	11	1	4½	64
Border	Blue-4		2½	40	7
Binding	Blue-4		2½	40	8

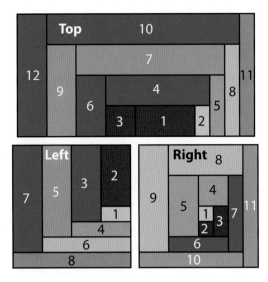

V8-V4 sewing sequence

Quilt Construction

Make 64 blocks following the V8-V4 piecing order given on pages 11–12.

The blocks (B) will be oriented by turning them once (B1), twice (B2), or three times (B3).

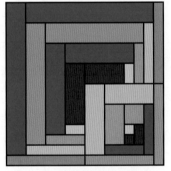 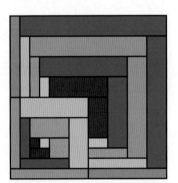 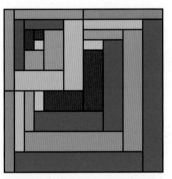 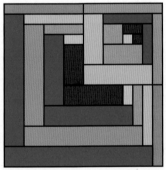

B: Block **B1: One turn clockwise** **B2: Two turns clockwise** **B3: Three turns clockwise**

Block orientation

Lay out the blocks in rows according to the quilt assembly diagram. Sew the blocks into rows and sew the rows together.

Cut 2 border strips 2½" x 64½" from blue-4. Sew to the sides of the quilt. Cut 2 border strips 2½" x 68½" from blue-4. Sew to the top and bottom of the quilt.

Layer and quilt according to your favorite method. Bind and label your quilt.

Quilt assembly

Voodoo Sunrise

Voodoo Sunrise, 52" x 68", pieced by Cindy Vognetz, Phoenixville, Pennsylvania, quilted by Barb Persing, Frederick, Pennsylvania (www.barbarapersing.com)

Block used: Valley8-Valley4 (V8-V4)

Number of blocks: 48 **Finished block size: 8" x 8"**

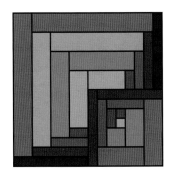

The V8-H4 block

Cindy had so much fun making the H4 units that she ended up with 10 extra. She was bound and determined to get them into the quilt, hence her delightfully original border. She used them in the center of 5½" Square-in-a-Square blocks and built the blocks into border strips slightly wider than are called for in the pattern.

The ½" (finished) angled strips were appliquéd in place. A ¼" flange, made from a folded 1" strip, was inserted between the quilt top and border.

Materials	
Orange-1: yard	Purple-1: ½ yard
Orange-2: ¾ yard	Purple-2: ½ yard
Orange-3: 1¼ yards	Purple-3: ½ yard
Orange-4: 1½ yards	Purple-4: 1½ yards (including border and binding)
Backing: 4¾ yards	Batting: 60" x 74"

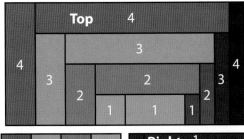

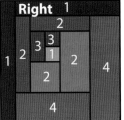

V8-H4 fabric selection

All measurements are in inches.					
V8-V4					
Section	Fabric	Piece	Width	Length	Cut
Top	Purple-1	2	1	1½	48
	Purple-2	5	1	2½	48
	Purple-3	8	1	3½	48
	Purple-4	11	1	4½	48
	Orange-1	1	1½	2½	48
	Orange-1	3	1½	1½	48
	Orange-2	4	1½	4	48
	Orange-2	6	1½	2½	48
	Orange-3	7	1½	5½	48
	Orange-3	9	1½	3½	48
	Orange-4	10	1½	7	48
	Orange-4	12	1½	4½	48
Left	Purple-1	1	1	1½	48
	Purple-2	4	1	2½	48
	Purple-3	6	1	3½	48
	Purple-4	8	1	4½	48
	Orange-1	2	1½	2½	48
	Orange-2	3	1½	3	48
	Orange-3	5	1½	3½	48
	Orange-4	7	1½	4	48
Right	Orange-1	1	1	1	48
	Orange-2	4	1½	1½	48
	Orange-2	5	1½	2½	48
	Orange-4	8	1½	3	48
	Orange-4	9	1½	4	48
	Purple-1	2	1	1	48
	Purple-1	3	1	1½	48
	Purple-2	6	1	2½	48
	Purple-2	7	1	3	48
	Purple-3	10	1	4	48
	Purple-3	11	1	4½	48
Border	Purple4		2½	40	7
Binding	Purple4		2½	40	8

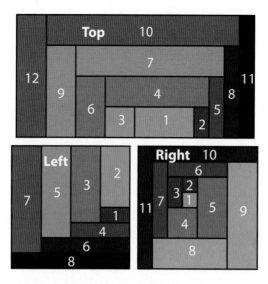

V8-H4 sewing sequence

Quilt Construction

Construct 48 blocks following the V8-H4 piecing sequence given on page 12.

The blocks (B) will be oriented by turning them once (B1), twice (B2), or three times (B3).

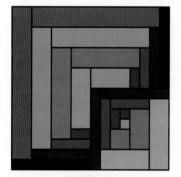 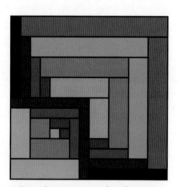 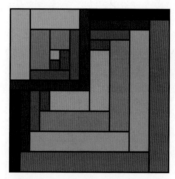 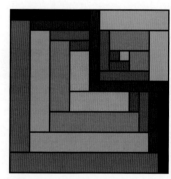

B: Block   **B1: One turn clockwise**   **B2: Two turns clockwise**   **B3: Three turns clockwise**

Block orientation

Lay out the blocks in rows according to the quilt assembly diagram. Sew the blocks into rows and sew the rows together.

Cut 2 border strips 2½" x 64½" from purple-4. Sew to the sides of the quilt. Cut 2 border strips 2½" x 52½" from purple-4. Sew to the top and bottom of the quilt.

Layer and quilt according to your favorite method. Bind and label your quilt.

Quilt assembly

Barn Raising

Barn Raising, 68" x 84", pieced and quilted by Robin McMillen, Downingtown, Pennsylvania

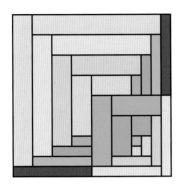

The V8-V4 block

The traditional Barn Raising set is used.

Materials

Pink-1: 1 yard	Turquoise-1: ⅞ yard
Pink-2: 1¼ yards	Turquoise-2: ⅞ yard
Pink-3: 1¾ yards	Turquoise-3: ¾ yard
Pink-4: 1½ yards	Turquoise-4: 1¾ yards (including border and binding)
Backing: 4½ yards	Batting: 76" x 92"

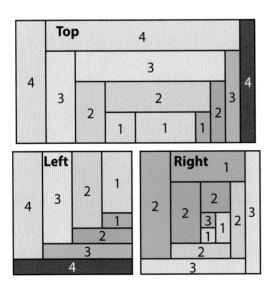

Fabric selection

Cutting Directions

All measurements are in inches.

V8-V4					
Section	**Fabric**	**Piece**	**Width**	**Length**	**Cut**
Top	Turquoise-1	2	1	1½	80
	Turquoise-2	5	1	2½	80
	Turquoise-3	8	1	3½	80
	Turquoise-4	11	1	4½	80
	Pink-1	1	1½	2½	80
	Pink-1	3	1½	1½	80
	Pink-2	4	1½	4	80
	Pink-2	6	1½	2½	80
	Pink-3	7	1½	5½	80
	Pink-3	9	1½	3½	80
	Pink-4	10	1½	7	80
	Pink-4	12	1½	4½	80
Left	Turquoise-1	1	1	1½	80
	Turquoise-2	4	1	2½	80
	Turquoise-3	6	1	3½	80
	Turquoise-4	8	1	4½	80
	Pink-1	2	1½	2½	80
	Pink-2	3	1½	3	80
	Pink-3	5	1½	3½	80
	Pink-4	7	1½	4	80
Right	Turquoise-3	1	1	1	80
	Turquoise-2	4	1½	1½	80
	Turquoise-2	5	1½	2½	80
	Turquoise-1	8	1½	3	80
	Turquoise-1	9	1½	4	80
	Pink-1	2	1	1	80
	Pink-1	3	1	1½	80
	Pink-2	6	1	2½	80
	Pink-2	7	1	3	80
	Pink-3	10	1	4	80
	Pink-3	11	1	4½	80
Border	Turquoise-4		2½	40	8
Binding	Turquoise-4		2½	40	8
Binding	Dark blue-3		2½	40	4

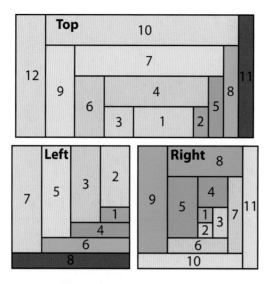

V8-V4 sewing sequence

Quilt Construction

Make 80 blocks following the V8-V4 piecing order given on pages 11–12.

The blocks (B) will be oriented by turning them once (B1), twice (B2), or three times (B3).

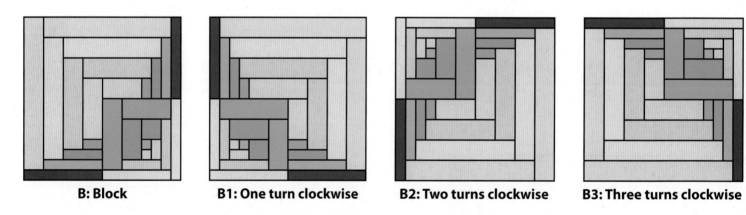

B: Block **B1: One turn clockwise** **B2: Two turns clockwise** **B3: Three turns clockwise**

Block orientation

Lay out the blocks in rows according to the quilt assembly diagram. Sew the blocks into rows and sew the rows together.

Cut 2 border strips 2½" x 80½" from turquoise-4. Sew to the sides of the quilt. Cut 2 border strips 2½" x 68½" from turquoise-4. Sew to the top and bottom of the quilt.

Layer and quilt according to your favorite method. Bind and label your quilt.

Quilt assembly

SUNBURST

SUNBURST, 36" x 36", pieced and quilted by the author

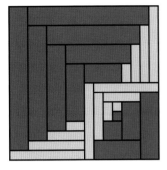

The V8-H4 block

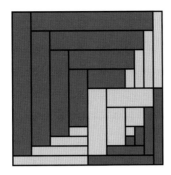

The V8-V4 block

This setting shows the circular effects of the V8-H4 block and the diamond effect of the V8-V4 block.

Materials

Blue: 1⅞ yards (including border and binding)	Backing: 1⅜ yards
Yellow: 1 yard	Batting: 40" x 40"

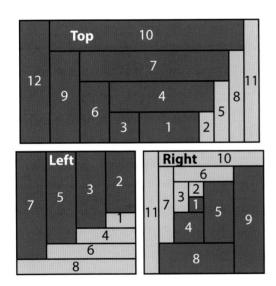

V8-H4 sewing sequence

Cutting Directions

All measurements are in inches.

V8-H4					
Section	Fabric	Piece	Width	Length	Cut
Top	Yellow	2	1	1½	12
	Yellow	5	1	2½	12
	Yellow	8	1	3½	12
	Yellow	11	1	4½	12
	Blue	1	1½	2½	12
	Blue	3	1½	1½	12
	Blue	4	1½	4	12
	Blue	6	1½	2½	12
	Blue	7	1½	5½	12
	Blue	9	1½	3½	12
	Blue	10	1½	7	12
	Blue	12	1½	4½	12
Left	Yellow	1	1	1½	12
	Yellow	4	1	2½	12
	Yellow	6	1	3½	12
	Yellow	8	1	4½	12
	Blue	2	1½	2½	12
	Blue	3	1½	3	12
	Blue	5	1½	3½	12
	Blue	7	1½	4	12
Right	Yellow	2	1	1	12
	Yellow	3	1	1½	12
	Yellow	6	1	2½	12
	Yellow	7	1	3	12
	Yellow	10	1	4	12
	Yellow	11	1	4½	12
	Blue	1	1	1	12
	Blue	4	1½	1½	12
	Blue	5	1½	2½	12
	Blue	8	1½	3	12
	Blue	9	1½	4	12
Border	Blue		2½	40	4
	Yellow		1½	40	4
Binding	Blue		2½	40	4

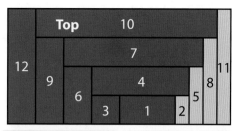

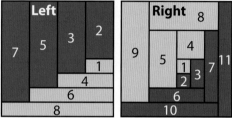

V8-V4 sewing sequence

A: Block

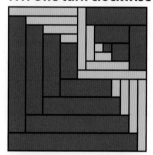

A1: One turn clockwise

A2: Two turns clockwise

A3: Three turns clockwise

B: Block

B1: One turn clockwise

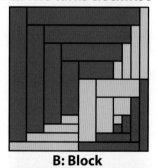

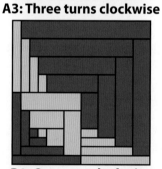

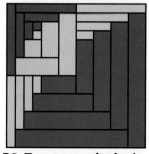

B2: Two turns clockwise

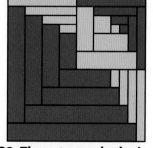

B3: Three turns clockwise

Block orientation

Cutting Directions

All measurements are in inches.

Section	Fabric	Piece	Width	Length	Cut
Top	Yellow	2	1	$1\frac{1}{2}$	4
	Yellow	5	1	$2\frac{1}{2}$	4
	Yellow	8	1	$3\frac{1}{2}$	4
	Yellow	11	1	$4\frac{1}{2}$	4
	Blue	1	$1\frac{1}{2}$	$2\frac{1}{2}$	4
	Blue	3	$1\frac{1}{2}$	$1\frac{1}{2}$	4
	Blue	4	$1\frac{1}{2}$	4	4
	Blue	6	$1\frac{1}{2}$	$2\frac{1}{2}$	4
	Blue	7	$1\frac{1}{2}$	$5\frac{1}{2}$	4
	Blue	9	$1\frac{1}{2}$	$3\frac{1}{2}$	4
	Blue	10	$1\frac{1}{2}$	7	4
	Blue	12	$1\frac{1}{2}$	$4\frac{1}{2}$	4
Left	Yellow	1	1	$1\frac{1}{2}$	4
	Yellow	4	1	$2\frac{1}{2}$	4
	Yellow	6	1	$3\frac{1}{2}$	4
	Yellow	8	1	$4\frac{1}{2}$	4
	Blue	2	$1\frac{1}{2}$	$2\frac{1}{2}$	4
	Blue	3	$1\frac{1}{2}$	3	4
	Blue	5	$1\frac{1}{2}$	$3\frac{1}{2}$	4
	Blue	7	$1\frac{1}{2}$	4	4
Right	Blue	2	1	1	4
	Blue	3	1	$1\frac{1}{2}$	4
	Blue	6	1	$2\frac{1}{2}$	4
	Blue	7	1	3	4
	Blue	10	1	4	4
	Blue	11	1	$4\frac{1}{2}$	4
	Yellow	1	1	1	4
	Yellow	4	$1\frac{1}{2}$	$1\frac{1}{2}$	4
	Yellow	5	$1\frac{1}{2}$	$2\frac{1}{2}$	4
	Yellow	8	$1\frac{1}{2}$	3	4
	Yellow	9	$1\frac{1}{2}$	4	4

Quilt Construction

Make 12 V8-H4 (A) and 4 V8-V4 (B) blocks following the piecing order given on pages 11–12.

The blocks (A & B) will be oriented by turning them once (A1, B1), twice (A2, B2), or three times (A3, B3).

Quilt assembly

Lay out the blocks in rows according to the quilt assembly diagram. Sew the blocks into rows and sew the rows together.

For the first border, cut 2 strips 1½" x 32½" from the yellow fabric. Sew to the sides of the quilt. Cut 2 strips 1½" x 34½" from the yellow fabric and sew to the top and bottom of the quilt.

For the second border, cut 2 strips 2½" x 34½" from the blue fabric. Sew to the sides of the quilt. Cut 2 strips 2½" x 38½" from the blue fabric and add to the top and bottom of the quilt.

Layer and quilt according to your favorite method. Bind and label your quilt.

ISLANDS IN THE STREAM, 52" x 68", designed, pieced, and quilted by the author

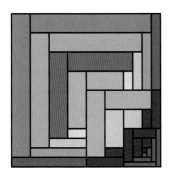

The V8-V4-V2 block

I design everything in EQ (Electric Quilt) and, being color blind, use only those colors that I can see—red, yellow, blue, and black. The blue suggested water, hence the title. This design is loosely based on the BARN RAISING set (see page 28).

When I made the quilt, I changed the colors, but left the name alone. This quilt requires 4 oranges, 4 aquas, and a teal.

Materials

Aqua-1: ½ yard	Orange-1: ½ yard
Aqua-2: ½ yard	Orange-2: ½ yard
Aqua-3: ¾ yard	Orange-3: ¾ yard
Aqua-4: 1 yard	Orange-4: 1 yard
Teal: 1½ yards (including border and binding)	Backing: 4½ yards
Batting: 60" x 76"	

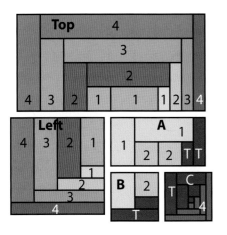

V8-V4-V2 fabric selection

Cutting Directions

All measurements are in inches.

V8-V4-V2					
Section	**Fabric**	**Piece**	**Width**	**Length**	**Cut**
Top	Aqua-1	2	1	1 ½	48
	Aqua-2	5	1	2½	48
	Aqua-3	8	1	3½	48
	Aqua-4	11	1	4½	48
	Orange-1	1	1½	2½	48
	Orange-1	3	1½	1½	48
	Orange-2	4	1½	4	48
	Orange-2	6	1½	2½	48
	Orange-3	7	1½	5½	48
	Orange-3	9	1½	3½	48
	Orange-4	10	1½	7	48
	Orange-4	12	1½	4½	48
Left	Aqua-1	1	1	1½	48
	Aqua-2	4	1	2½	48
	Aqua-3	6	1	3½	48
	Aqua-4	8	1	4½	48
	Orange-1	2	1½	2½	48
	Orange-2	3	1½	3	48
	Orange-3	5	1½	3½	48
	Orange-4	7	1½	4	48
A	Aqua-1	4	1½	3	48
	Aqua-1	6	1½	2½	48
	Aqua-2	1	1½	1½	48
	Aqua-2	3	1½	1½	48
	Teal	2	1	1½	48
	Teal	5	1	2½	48
B	Teal	1	1	1½	48
	Teal	4	1	2½	48
	Aqua-1	3	1½	2	48
	Aqua-2	2	1½	1½	48
C	Teal	1	¾	¾	48
	Teal	4	1	1	48
	Teal	5	1	1½	48
	Teal	8	1	1¾	48
	Teal	9	1	2¼	48

V8-V4-V2 (cont.)					
Section	Fabric	Piece	Width	Length	Cut
	Aqua-4	2	¾	¾	48
	Aqua-4	3	¾	1	48
	Aqua-4	6	¾	1½	48
	Aqua-4	7	¾	1¾	48
	Aqua-4	10	¾	2¼	48
	Aqua-4	11	¾	2½	48
Border	Teal		2½	40	2
	Teal		2½	40	2
Binding	Aqua-4		2½	40	7

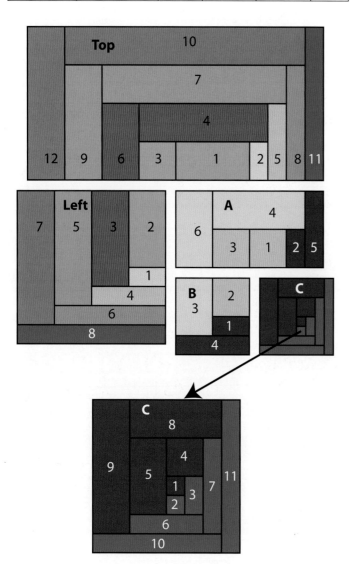

Sewing sequence

Quilt Construction

Make 48 V8-V4-V2 blocks following the piecing order given on pages 13–14.

The blocks (B) are oriented by turning them clockwise once (B1), twice (B2), or three times (B3).

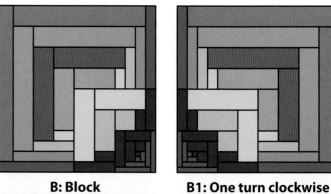

B: Block   **B1: One turn clockwise**

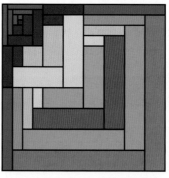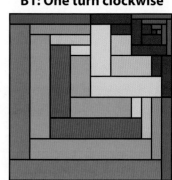

B2: Two turns clockwise   **B3: Three turns clockwise**

Block orientation

Lay out the blocks out in rows according to the quilt assembly diagram. Sew the blocks into rows and sew the rows together.

Cut 2 border strips 2½" x 64½" from the teal. Sew to the sides of the quilt. Cut 2 border strips 2½" x 52½" from the teal. Sew to the top and bottom of the quilt.

Layer and quilt according to your favorite method. Bind and label your quilt.

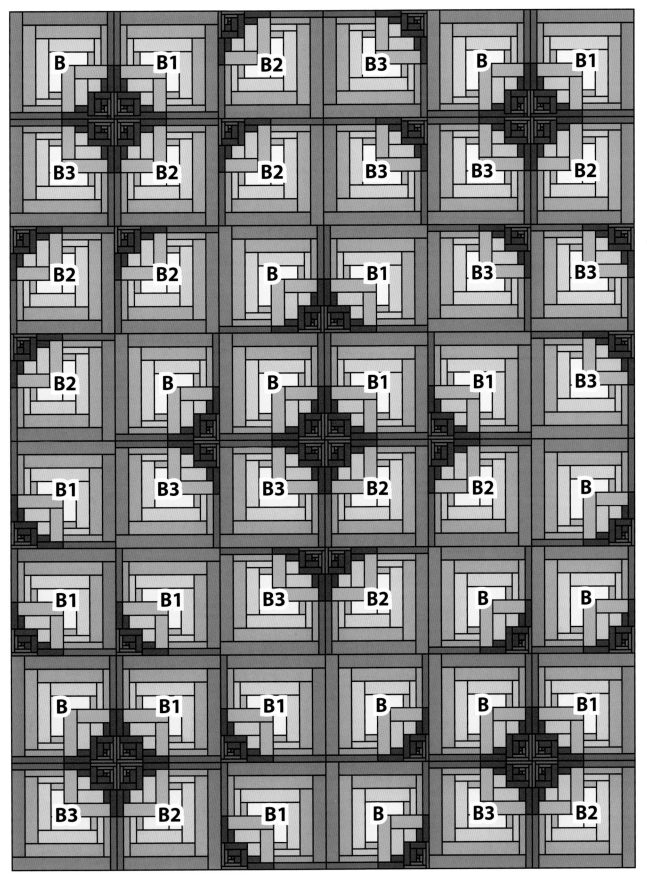

Quilt assembly

DIAMOND STAR

DIAMOND STAR, 68" x 68", pieced by Myrna Paluba, Wayne, Pennsylvania,
quilted by Carol Lee Heisler, Lorac Designs, East Norriton, Pennsylvania

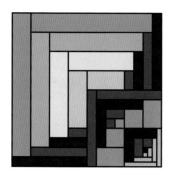

The V8-H4-V2 block

Myrna's placement of the colors within the blocks results in orange circles in the diamonds, with small orange diamonds in the circles. This quilt requires 4 light blues, 2 dark blues, and 2 oranges.

Materials

Dark blue-1: 1¼ yards	Light blue-1: ½ yard
Dark blue-2: 2½ yards (including binding)	Light blue-2: ¾ yard
Orange-1: ¾ yard	Light blue-3: 1 yard
Orange-2: ½ yard	Light blue-4: 1¼ yards
Backing: 4½ yards	Batting: 76" x 76"

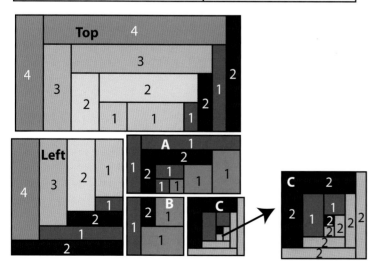

V8-H4-V2 fabric selection

Cutting Directions

All measurements are in inches.

V8-H4-V2					
Section	Fabric	Piece	Width	Length	Cut
Top	Dark blue-1	2	1	1½	64
	Dark blue-1	8	1	3½	64
	Dark blue-2	5	1	2½	64
	Dark blue-2	11	1	4½	64
	Light blue-1	1	1½	2½	64
	Light blue-1	3	1½	1½	64
	Light blue-2	4	1½	4	64
	Light blue-2	6	1½	2½	64
	Light blue-3	7	1½	5½	64
	Light blue-3	9	1½	3½	64
	Light blue-4	10	1½	7	64
	Light blue-4	12	1½	4½	64
Left	Dark blue-1	1	1	1½	64
	Dark blue-1	6	1	3½	64
	Dark blue-2	4	1	2½	64
	Dark blue-2	8	1	4½	64
	Light blue-1	2	1½	2½	64
	Light blue-2	3	1½	3	64
	Light blue-3	5	1½	3½	64
	Light blue-4	7	1½	4	64
A	Dark blue-1	2	1	1	64
	Dark blue-1	3	1	1½	64
	Dark blue-1	8	1	4	64
	Dark blue-1	9	1	2½	64
	Dark blue-2	5	1	2½	64
	Dark blue-2	6	1	2	64
	Orange-1	1	1	1	64
	Orange-1	4	1½	1½	64
	Orange-1	7	1½	2	64
B	Dark blue-1	4	1	2½	64
	Dark blue-2	2	1	1½	64
	Orange-1	1	1½	1½	64
	Orange-1	3	1½	2	64
C	Dark blue-1	4	1	1	64
	Dark blue-1	5	1½	1½	64
	Dark blue-2	1	¾	¾	64

V8-H4-V2 (cont.)					
Section	**Fabric**	**Piece**	**Width**	**Length**	**Cut**
	Dark blue-2	8	1½	1¾	64
	Dark blue-2	9	1½	2¼	64
	Orange-2	2	¾	¾	64
	Orange-2	3	¾	1	64
	Orange-2	6	¾	1½	64
	Orange-2	7	¾	1¾	64
	Orange-2	10	¾	2¼	64
	Orange-2	11	¾	2½	64
Border	Dark blue-2		2½	40	7
Binding	Dark blue-2		2½	40	7

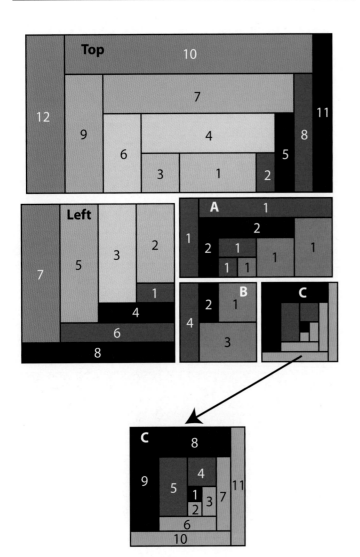

V8-H4-V2 fabric placement

Quilt Construction

Make 64 V8-H4-V2 blocks following the piecing order given on page 14.

The blocks (B) are oriented by turning them clockwise once (B1), twice (B2), or three times (B3).

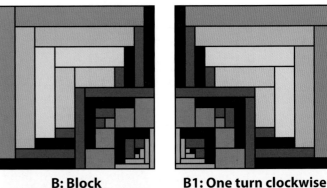

B: Block   **B1: One turn clockwise**

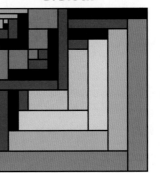
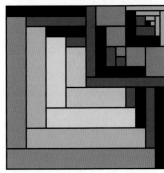

B2: Two turns clockwise   **B3: Three turns clockwise**

Block orientation

Lay out the blocks in rows according to the quilt assembly diagram. Sew the blocks into rows and sew the rows together.

Layer and quilt according to your favorite method. Bind and label your quilt.

Quilt assembly

CHOCOLATE & CARAMEL, 68" x 68", pieced by Sara Borr, Downingtown, Pennsylvania,
quilted by Carol Lee Heisler, Lorac Designs, East Norriton, Pennsylvania

The V8-H4-V2 block

The same block as was used in Diamond Star (page 40) takes on a different look in the traditional Figure Eight setting. It requires 4 tans, 3 dark browns, and 4 beiges.

Materials

Tan-1: ½ yard	Beige-3: ½ yard
Tan-2: ⅞ yard	Beige-4: ½ yard
Tan-3: 1⅛ yards	Dark brown-1: ¼ yard
Tan-4: 1¼ yards	Dark brown-2: ½ yard
Beige-1: ¾ yard	Dark brown-3: 1½ yards (including border and binding)
Beige-2: ⅝ yard	Backing: 4½ yards
Batting: 76" x 76"	

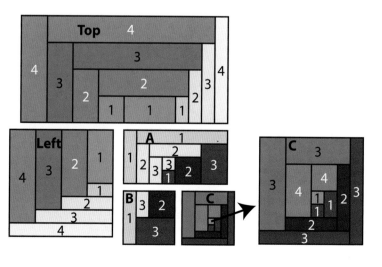

V8-H4-V2 fabric selection

Cutting Directions

All measurements are in inches.

Section	Fabric	Piece	Width	Length	Cut
V8-H4-V2					
Top	Beige-1	2	1	1½	64
	Beige-2	5	1	2½	64
	Beige-3	8	1	3½	64
	Beige-4	11	1	4½	64
	Tan-1	1	1½	2½	64
	Tan-1	3	1½	1½	64
	Tan-2	4	1½	4	64
	Tan-2	6	1½	2½	64
	Tan-3	7	1½	5½	64
	Tan-3	9	1½	3½	64
	Tan-4	10	1½	7	64
	Tan-4	12	1½	4½	64
Left	Beige-1	1	1	1½	64
	Beige-2	4	1	2½	64
	Beige-3	6	1	3½	64
	Beige-4	8	1	4½	64
	Tan-1	2	1½	2½	64
	Tan-2	3	1½	3	64
	Tan-3	5	1½	3½	64
	Tan-4	7	1½	4	64
A	Beige-3	2	1	1	64
	Beige-3	3	1	1½	64
	Beige-2	5	1	2½	64
	Beige-2	6	1	2	64
	Beige-1	8	1	4	64
	Beige-1	9	1	2½	64
	Dark brown-1	1	1	1	64
	Dark brown-2	4	1½	1½	64
	Dark brown-3	7	1½	2	64
B	Beige-2	2	1	1½	64
	Beige-1	4	1	2½	64
	Dark brown-2	1	1½	1½	64
	Dark brown-3	3	1½	2	64
C	Dark brown-1	2	¾	¾	64
	Dark brown-1	3	¾	1	64
	Dark brown-2	6	¾	1½	64

Section	Fabric	Piece	Width	Length	Cut
V8-H4-V2 (cont.)					
	Dark brown-2	7	¾	1¾	64
	Dark brown-3	10	¾	2¼	64
	Dark brown-3	11	¾	2½	64
	Beige-1	1	¾	¾	64
	Beige-2	4	1	1	64
	Beige-2	5	1	1½	64
	Beige-3	8	1	1¾	64
	Beige-3	9	1	2¼	64
Border	Dark brown-3		2½	40	7
Binding	Dark brown-3		2½	40	8

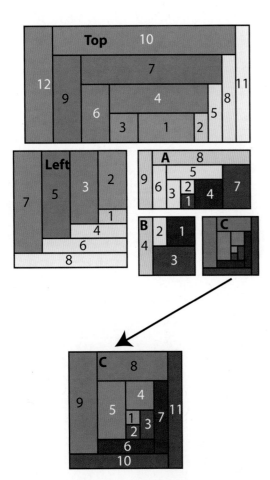

V8-H4-V2 fabric placement

Quilt Construction

Make 64 V8-H4-V2 blocks following the piecing order given on page 14.

The blocks (B) are oriented by turning them clockwise once (B1), twice (B2), or three times (B3).

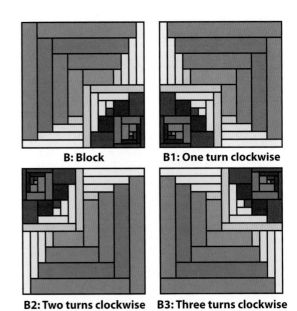

B: Block **B1: One turn clockwise**

B2: Two turns clockwise **B3: Three turns clockwise**

Block orientation

Cut 2 border strips 2½" x 64½" from dark brown-3. Sew to the sides of the quilt. Cut 2 border strips 2½" x 68½" from dark brown-3. Sew to the top and bottom of the quilt.

Layer and quilt according to your favorite method. Bind and label your quilt.

FIGURE EIGHT, 68" x 68", pieced by Fay Ann Grider, Gulph Mills, Pennsylvania, and quilted by Carol Lee Heisler, Lorac Designs, East Norriton, Pennsylvania. Fay Ann chose the Figure Eight setting but used the V8-V4-V2 block in place of the V8-H4-V2 block. This simple change produced a strikingly different quilt. She used a light raspberry next to a light teal-blue to maintain the essential "squareness" of the design and to contrast with the "curviness" of the block.

Quilt assembly

OUTER BANKS

OUTER BANKS, 36" x 36", designed by the author, pieced by Jean Fox, West Chester, Pennsylvania, quilted by Pat Smith, Media, Pennsylvania

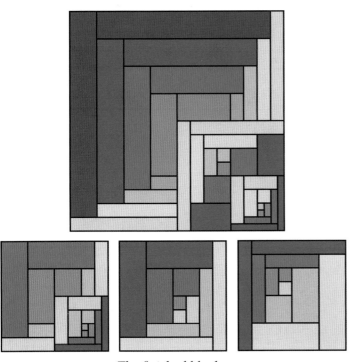

The finished blocks

This quilt illustrates the great versatility of the Hill & Valley Log Cabin blocks. It uses V8-H4-V2 blocks for the center medallion (the same block as used in Diamond Star page 40), V4-V2 blocks in the corners, and a combination of V4 and H4 blocks along the sides. It requires 4 blues and 4 yellows.

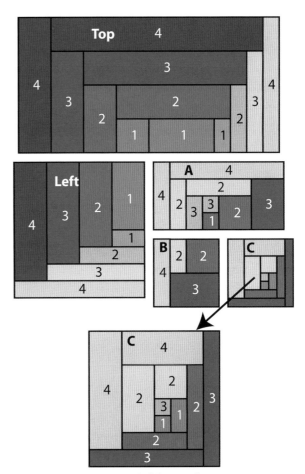

V8-H4-V2 fabric selection

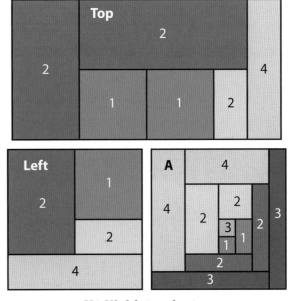

V4-V2 fabric selection

Materials

Blue-1: ⅜ yard	Yellow-2: ⅜ yard
Blue-2: ½ yard	Yellow-3: ⅜ yard
Blue-3: ½ yard	Yellow-4: ⅜ yard
Blue-4: ¾ yard (including border and binding)	Backing: 1¼ yards
Yellow-1: ¼ yard	Batting: 44" x 44"

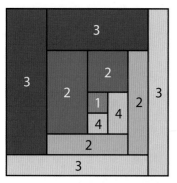

V4 fabric selection

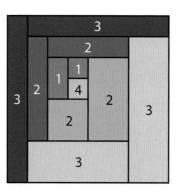

H4 fabric selection

Cutting Directions

All measurements are in inches.

V8-H4-V2					
Section	**Fabric**	**Piece**	**Width**	**Length**	**Cut**
Top	Yellow-1	2	1	1½	4
	Yellow-2	5	1	2½	4
	Yellow-3	8	1	3½	4
	Yellow-4	11	1	4½	4
	Blue-1	1	1½	2½	4
	Blue-1	3	1½	1½	4
	Blue-2	4	1½	4	4
	Blue-2	6	1½	2½	4
	Blue-3	7	1½	5½	4
	Blue-3	9	1½	3½	4
	Blue-4	10	1½	7	4
	Blue-4	12	1½	4½	4
Left	Yellow-1	1	1	1½	4
	Yellow-2	4	1	2½	4
	Yellow-3	6	1	3½	4
	Yellow-4	8	1	4½	4
	Blue-1	2	1½	2½	4
	Blue-2	3	1½	3	4
	Blue-3	5	1½	3½	4
	Blue-4	7	1½	4	4
A	Yellow-3	2	1	1	4
	Yellow-3	3	1	1½	4
	Yellow-2	5	1	2½	4
	Yellow-2	6	1	2	4
	Yellow-4	8	1	4	4
	Yellow-4	9	1	2½	4
	Blue-1	1	1	1	4
	Blue-2	4	1½	1½	4
	Blue-3	7	1½	2	4

B	Yellow-3	2	1	1½	4
	Yellow-4	4	1	2½	4
	Blue-2	1	1½	1½	4
	Blue-3	3	1½	2	4
C	Blue-1	2	¾	¾	4
	Blue-1	3	¾	1	4
	Blue-2	6	¾	1½	4
	Blue-2	7	¾	1¾	4
	Blue-3	10	¾	2¼	4
	Blue-3	11	¾	2½	4
	Yellow-3	1	¾	¾	4
	Yellow-2	4	1	1	4
	Yellow-2	5	1	1½	4
	Yellow-4	8	1	1¾	4
	Yellow-4	9	1	2 ¼	4
Border	Blue-4		2½	40	4
Binding	Blue-4		2½	40	4

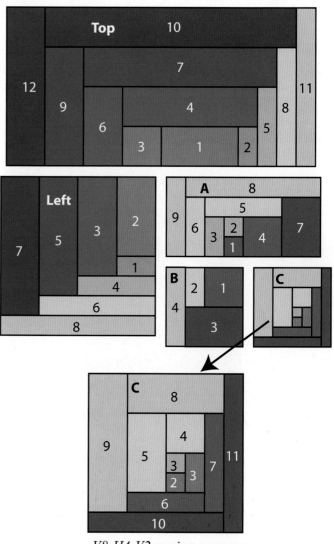

V8-H4-V2 sewing sequence

V4-V2					
Section	Fabric	Piece	Width	Length	Cut
Top	Yellow-2	2	1	1½	16
	Yellow-4	5	1	2½	16
	Blue-1	1	1½	1½	16
	Blue-1	3	1½	1½	16
	Blue-2	4	1½	3	16
	Blue-2	6	1½	2½	16
Left	Yellow-2	1	1	1½	16
	Yellow-4	4	1	2½	16
	Blue-1	2	1½	1½	16
	Blue-2	3	1½	2	16
A	Yellow-3	1	¾	¾	16
	Yellow-2	4	1	1	16
	Yellow-2	5	1	1½	16
	Yellow-4	8	1	1¾	16
	Yellow-4	9	1	2¼	16
	Blue-1	2	¾	¾	16
	Blue-1	3	¾	1	16
	Blue-2	6	¾	1½	16
	Blue-2	7	¾	1¾	16
	Blue-3	10	¾	2¼	16
	Blue-3	11	¾	2½	16

V4				
Fabric	Piece	Width	Length	Cut
Yellow-4	2	1	1	16
Yellow-4	3	1	1½	16
Yellow-2	6	1	2½	16
Yellow-2	7	1	3	16
Yellow-1	10	1	4	16
Yellow-1	11	1	4 ½	16
Blue-1	1	1	1	16
Blue-2	4	1½	1½	16
Blue-2	5	1½	2½	16
Blue-3	8	1½	3	16
Blue-3	9	1½	4	16

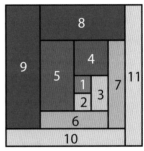

V4 sewing sequence

H4				
Fabric	Piece	Width	Length	Cut
Yellow-4	1	1	1	16
Yellow-2	4	1½	1½	16
Yellow-2	5	1½	2½	16
Yellow-1	8	1½	3	16
Yellow-1	9	1½	4	16
Blue-1	2	1	1	16
Blue-1	3	1	1½	16
Blue-2	6	1	2½	16
Blue-2	7	1	3	16
Blue-3	10	1	4	16
Blue-3	11	1	4½	16

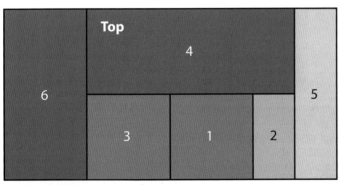

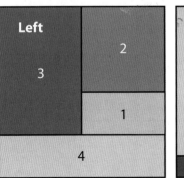

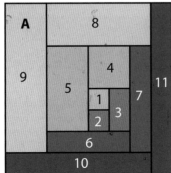

V4-V2 sewing sequence

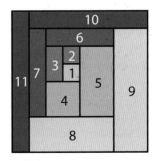

H4 sewing sequence

Quilt Construction

The quilt is constructed in nine sections. The blocks are turned once, twice, or three times clockwise to construct the various sections.

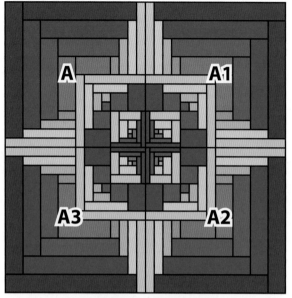

Center medallion

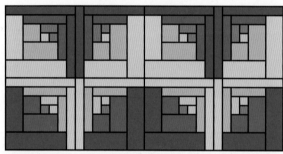

Side unit

Corner

Center medallion

Make 4 – V8-H4-V2 blocks. Position the blocks with the V2 portion toward the center, turning each block once clockwise to form the medallion. Join the 4 blocks.

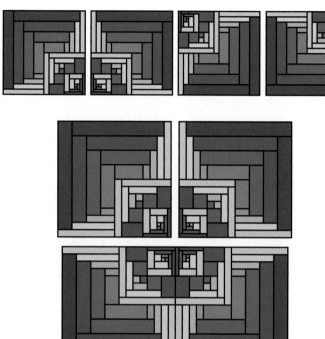

Joining the V8-H4-V2 blocks

Sides

Make 16 – H4 blocks and 16 – V4 blocks.

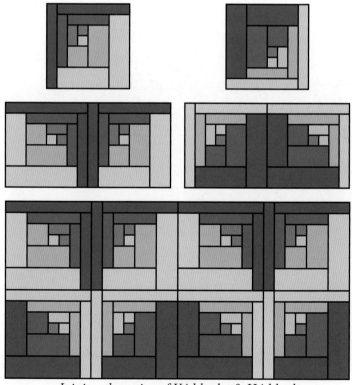

Joining the pairs of V4 blocks & H4 blocks

Corners

Make 16 – V4-V2 blocks. For each corner section, position 4 blocks with the V2 portion toward the center, turning each block once clockwise to form the corner unit. Join the 4 blocks. Make 4 corner units.

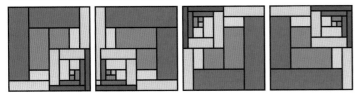

Joining the V4-V2 blocks

Joining the units

Lay out the center medallion, corners, and side sections according to the quilt assembly diagram, turning the side units clockwise as you place them around the center.

Join the units into 3 rows, then join the rows.

Cut 2 border strips 2½" x 32½" from blue-4. Sew to the sides of the quilt. Cut 2 border strips 2½" x 36½" from blue-4. Sew to the top and bottom of the quilt.

Layer and quilt according to your favorite method. Bind and label your quilt.

Quilt assembly

RESURRECTION

RESURRECTION, 52" x 68", pieced by Rob Lodi and quilted by Pat Smith, both of Downingtown, Pennsylvania

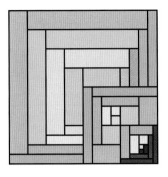
Block A – Make 36

Block B – Make 12

This is the traditional God's Cross setting using two colorings of the V8-H4-V2 block. The color combinations suggest an Art Deco look. It requires 4 greens, 4 grays, and 4 blacks.

Materials

Green-1: ⅜ yard	Gray-4: ½ yard
Green-2: ¾ yard	Black-1: ¼ yard
Green-3: ⅞ yard	Black-2: ¼ yard
Green-4: ¾ yard	Black-3: ⅜ yard
Gray-1: ⅝ yard	Black-4: 1⅜ yards (including border and binding)
Gray-2: ⅝ yard	Backing: 4½ yards
Gray-3: ⅝ yard	Batting: 60" x 76"

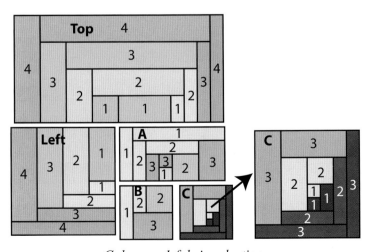
Colorway 1 fabric selection

Cutting Directions

All measurements are in inches.

Colorway 1 – V8-H4-V2					
Section	**Fabric**	**Piece**	**Width**	**Length**	**Cut**
Top	Gray-1	2	1	1½	36
	Gray-2	5	1	2½	36
	Gray-3	8	1	3½	36
	Gray-4	11	1	4½	36
	Green-1	1	1½	2½	36
	Green-1	3	1½	1½	36
	Green-2	4	1½	4	36
	Green-2	6	1½	2½	36
	Green-3	7	1½	5½	36
	Green-3	9	1½	3½	36
	Green-4	10	1½	7	36
	Green-4	12	1½	4½	36
Left	Gray-1	1	1	1½	36
	Gray-2	4	1	2½	36
	Gray-3	6	1	3½	36
	Gray-4	8	1	4½	36
	Green-1	2	1½	2½	36
	Green-2	3	1½	3	36
	Green-3	5	1½	3½	36
	Green-4	7	1½	4	36
A	Gray-3	2	1	1	36
	Gray-3	3	1	1½	36
	Gray-2	5	1	2½	36
	Gray-2	6	1	2	36
	Gray-1	8	1	4	36
	Gray-1	9	1	2½	36
	Green-1	1	1	1	36
	Green-2	4	1½	1½	36
	Green-3	7	1½	2	36
B	Gray-2	2	1	1½	36
	Gray-1	4	1	2½	36
	Green-2	1	1½	1½	36
	Green-3	3	1½	2	36
C	Black-1	2	¾	¾	36
	Black-1	3	¾	1	36

Colorway 1 – V8-H4-V2 (cont.)					
Section	Fabric	Piece	Width	Length	Cut
	Black-2	6	¾	1½	36
	Black-2	7	¾	1¾	36
	Black-3	10	¾	2¼	36
	Black-3	11	¾	2½	36
	Gray-1	1	¾	¾	36
	Gray-2	4	1	1	36
	Gray-2	5	1	1½	36
	Gray-3	8	1	1¾	36
	Gray-3	9	1	2¼	36

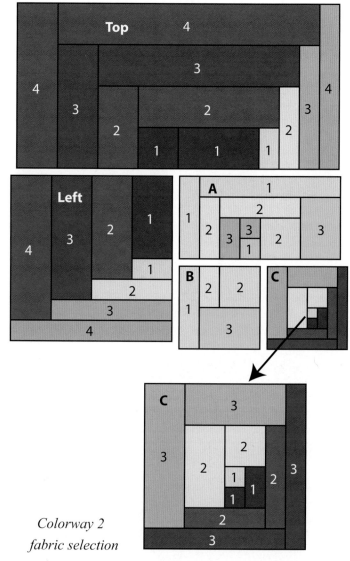

Colorway 2
fabric selection

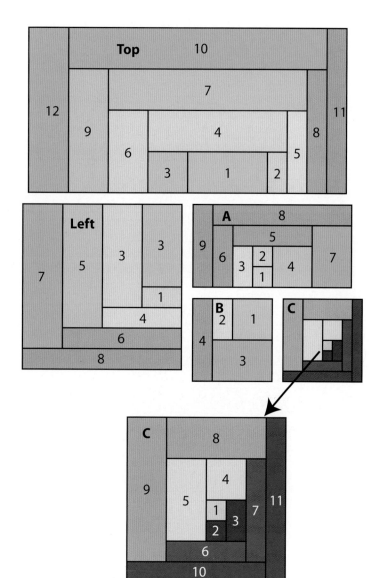

Colorway 1 sewing sequence

Colorway 2 – V8-H4-V2					
Section	Fabric	Piece	Width	Length	Cut
Top	Gray-1	2	1	1½	12
	Gray-2	5	1	2½	12
	Gray-3	8	1	3½	12
	Gray-4	11	1	4½	12
	Black-1	1	1½	2½	12
	Black-1	3	1½	1½	12
	Black-2	4	1½	4	12
	Black-2	6	1½	2½	12
	Black-3	7	1½	5½	12
	Black-3	9	1½	3½	12
	Black-4	10	1½	7	12
	Black-4	12	1½	4½	12
Left	Gray-1	1	1	1½	12
	Gray-2	4	1	2½	12
	Gray-3	6	1	3½	12

	Gray-4	8	1	4½	12
	Black-1	2	1½	2½	12
	Black -2	3	1½	3	12
	Black -3	5	1½	3½	12
	Black -4	7	1½	4	12
A	Gray-3	2	1	1	12
	Gray-3	3	1	1½	12
	Gray-2	5	1	2½	12
	Gray-2	6	1	2	12
	Gray-1	8	1	4	12
	Gray-1	9	1	2½	12
	Green-1	1	1	1	12
	Green-2	4	1½	1½	12
	Green-3	7	1½	2	12
B	Gray-2	2	1	1½	12
	Gray-1	4	1	2½	12
	Green-2	1	1½	1½	12
	Green-3	3	1½	2	12
C	Black-1	2	¾	¾	12
	Black-1	3	¾	1	12
	Black-2	6	¾	1½	12
	Black-2	7	¾	1¾	12
	Black-3	10	¾	2 ¼	12
	Black-3	11	¾	2½	12
	Gray-1	1	¾	¾	12
	Gray-2	4	1	1	12
	Gray-2	5	1	1½	12
	Gray-3	8	1	1¾	12
	Gray-3	9	1	2¼	12
Border	Black-4		2½	40	7
Binding	Black-4		2½	40	8

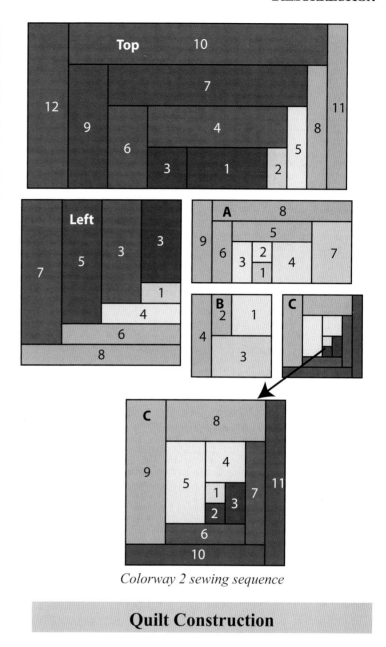

Colorway 2 sewing sequence

Quilt Construction

Make 36 Block A in colorway 1 and 12 Block B in colorway 2 following the piecing order given on page 14.

The blocks (A & B) are oriented by turning them clockwise once (A1 & B1), twice (A2 & B2), or three times (A3 & B3).

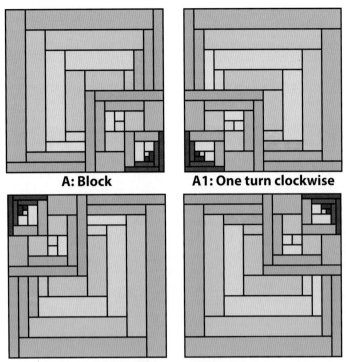

A: Block　　　**A1: One turn clockwise**

A2: Two turns clockwise　　**A3: Three turns clockwise**

Block orientation

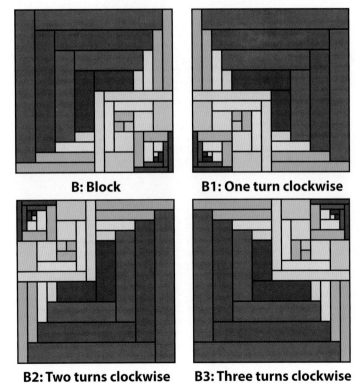

B: Block　　　**B1: One turn clockwise**

B2: Two turns clockwise　　**B3: Three turns clockwise**

Block orientation

Lay out the blocks out in rows according to the quilt assembly diagram. Sew the blocks into rows and sew the rows together.

Cut 2 border strips 2½" x 64½" from black-4. Sew to the sides of the quilt. Cut 2 border strips 2½" x 52½" from black-4. Sew to the top and bottom of the quilt.

Layer and quilt according to your favorite method. Bind and label your quilt.

Quilt assembly

TURKISH FLOOR

TURKISH FLOOR, 68" x 68", designed by the author, pieced and quilted by Kathleen DeCarli, Downingtown, Pennsylvania

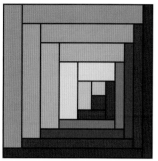

V8 block – Make 36 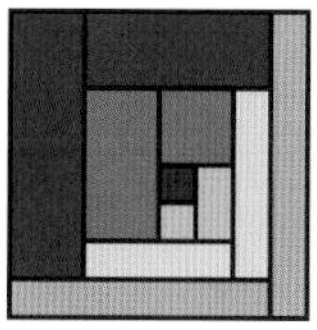   *V4 block – Make 112*

The combination of the two sizes of the same block makes this dramatic design possible. It requires 5 plums and 5 greens.

Materials

Plum-1: ⅜ yard	Green-1: ½ yard
Plum-2: ¾ yard	Green-2: ⅞ yard
Plum-3: 1¼ yards	Green-3: 1¼ yards
Plum-4: ½ yard	Green-4: ⅝ yard
Plum-5: 1½ yards (including border and binding)	Green-5: ¾ yard
Batting: 76" x 76"	Backing: 4½ yards

Cutting Directions

All measurements are in inches.

V8				
Fabric	**Piece**	**Width**	**Length**	**Cut**
Plum-1	1	1¼	1¼	36
Plum-1	4	1	2	36
Plum-1	5	1	2½	36
Plum-2	8	1	3½	36
Plum-2	9	1	4	36
Plum-3	12	1	5	36
Plum-3	13	1	5½	36
Plum-4	16	1	6½	36
Plum-4	17	1	7	36
Plum-5	20	1	8	36
Plum-5	21	1	8½	36
Plum-5	Border / Binding	2½	40	13
Green-1	2	1¼	1¼	36
Green-1	3	1¼	2	36
Green-2	6	1½	2½	36
Green-2	7	1½	3½	36
Green-3	10	1½	4	36
Green-3	11	1½	5	36
Green-4	14	1½	5½	36
Green-4	15	1½	6½	36
Green-5	18	1½	7	36
Green-5	19	1½	8	36

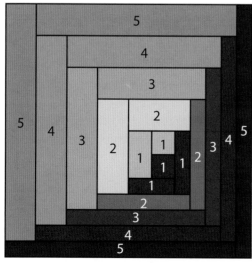

Fabric selection

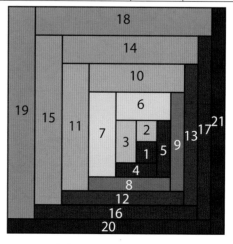

V8 sewing sequence

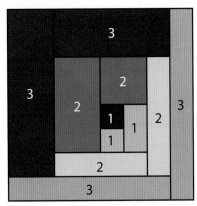

Fabric selection

V4				
Fabric	**Piece**	**Width**	**Length**	**Cut**
Plum-1	1	1	1	112
Plum-2	4	1½	1½	112
Plum-2	5	1½	2½	112
Plum-3	8	1½	3	112
Plum-3	9	1½	4	112
Green-1	2	1	1	112
Green-1	3	1	1½	112
Green-2	6	1	2½	112
Green-2	7	1	3	112
Green-3	10	1	4	112
Green-3	11	1	4½	112

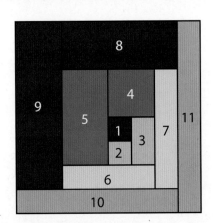

V4 sewing sequence

Quilt Construction

Make 36 V8 blocks and 112 V4 blocks following the piecing order given on pages 10–11.

Make units of 4 – V4 blocks by turning the blocks once, twice, or three times clockwise, positioning the valley portion of the block toward the center. Make 28 units (B).

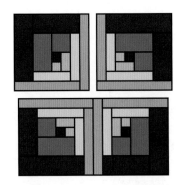

The V4 units – Make 28

The V8 blocks are turned once, twice, or three times to construct the quilt.

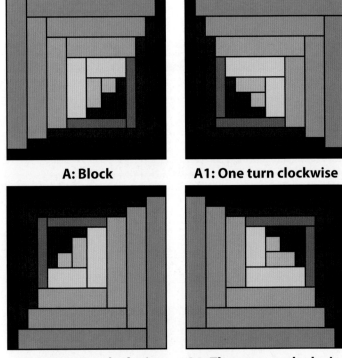

A: Block   **A1: One turn clockwise**

A2: Two turns clockwise   **A3: Three turns clockwise**

V8 block orientation

Lay out the V8 blocks and V4 units in rows according to the quilt assembly diagram. Sew the blocks into rows and sew the rows together.

Cut 2 border strips 2½" x 64½" from plum-5. Sew to the sides of the quilt. Cut 2 border strips 2½" x 68½" from plum-5. Sew to the top and bottom of the quilt.

Layer and quilt according to your favorite method. Bind and label your quilt.

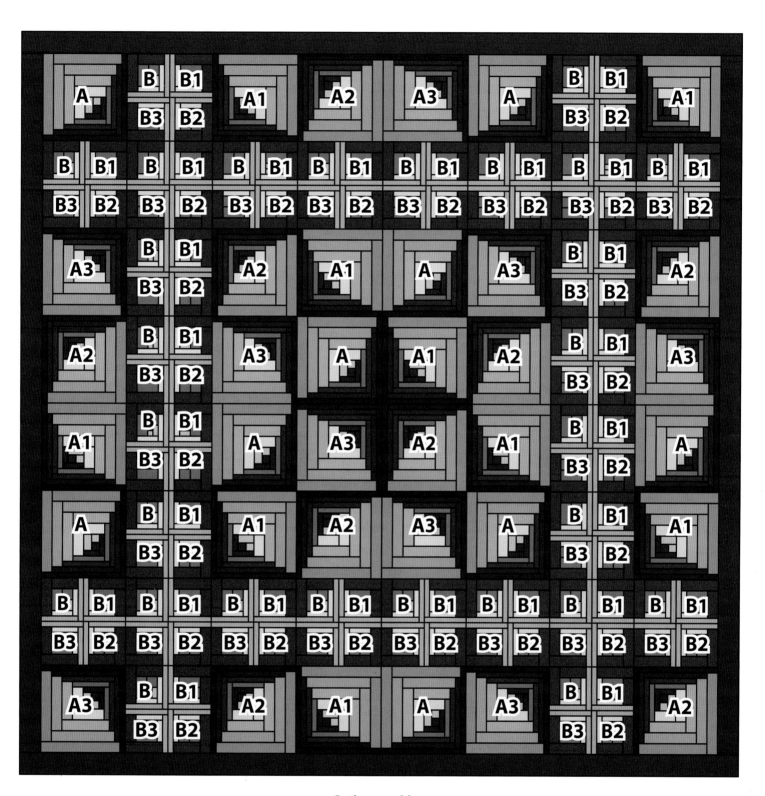

Quilt assembly

ZIGZAG DIAMOND, 52" x 68", pieced by Kelly Meanix, Downingtown, Pennsylvania, quilted by Susie Racobaldo, Kennett Square, Pennsylvania

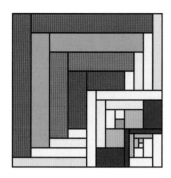

V8-H4-H2 block – Make 48

The traditional Zigzag Diamond setting features the V8-H4-H2 block. Kelly used the green color family to highlight the zigzag design. It requires 4 pinks, 4 white prints, and 3 greens.

Materials

Pink-1: ½ yard	White print-3: ⅝ yard
Pink-2: ½ yard	White print-4: 1 yard
Pink-3: ¾ yard	Green-1: ¼ yard
Pink-4: 2 yards (including border and binding)	Green-2: ⅜ yard
White print-1: ⅜ yard	Green-3: ½ yard
White print-2: ½ yard	Backing: 4½ yards
Batting: 60" x 76"	

Fabric selection

Cutting Directions

All measurements are in inches.

Section	Fabric	Piece	Width	Length	Cut
V8-H4-H2					
Top	White print-1	2	1	1½	48
	White print-2	5	1	2½	48
	White print-3	8	1	3½	48
	White print-4	11	1	4½	48
	Pink-1	1	1½	2½	48
	Pink-1	3	1½	1½	48
	Pink-2	4	1½	4	48
	Pink-2	6	1½	2½	48
	Pink-3	7	1½	5½	48
	Pink-3	9	1½	3½	48
	Pink-4	10	1½	7	48
	Pink-5	12	1½	4½	48
Left	White print-1	1	1	1½	48
	White print-2	4	1	2½	48
	White print-3	6	1	3½	48
	White print-4	8	1	4½	48
	Pink-1	2	1½	2½	48
	Pink-2	3	1½	3	48
	Pink-3	5	1½	3½	48
	Pink-4	7	1½	4	48
A	White print-2	2	1	1	48
	White print-2	3	1	1½	48
	White print-3	5	1	2½	48
	White print-3	6	1	2	48
	White print-4	8	1	4	48
	White print-4	9	1	2½	48
	Green-1	1	1	1	48
	Green-2	4	1½	1½	48
	Green-3	7	1½	2	48
B	White print-3	2	1	1½	48
	White print-4	4	1	2½	48
	Green-2	1	1½	1½	48
	Green-3	3	1½	2	48
C	White print-2	1	¾	¾	48

V8-H4-H2					
Section	Fabric	Piece	Width	Length	Cut
	White print-3	4	1	1	48
	White print-3	5	1	1½	48
	White print-4	8	1	1¾	48
	White print-4	9	1	2¼	48
	Green-1	2	¾	¾	48
	Green-1	3	¾	1	48
	Green-2	6	¾	1½	48
	Green-2	7	¾	1¾	48
	Green-3	10	¾	2¼	48
	Green-3	11	¾	2½	48
Border	Pink-4		2½	40	6
Binding	Pink-4		2½	40	7

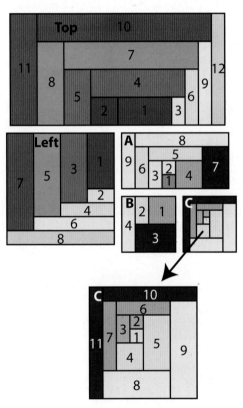

Sewing sequence

Quilt Construction

Make 48 V8-H4-H2 blocks (B) following the piecing order given on page 14.

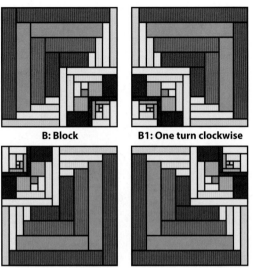

B: Block **B1: One turn clockwise**

B2: Two turns clockwise **B3: Three turns clockwise**

Block orientation

Lay out the blocks in rows according to the quilt assembly diagram. Sew the blocks into rows and sew the rows together.

Cut 2 border strips 2½" x 64½" from pink-4. Sew to the sides of the quilt. Cut 2 border strips 2½" x 52½" from pink-4. Sew to the top and bottom of the quilt.

Layer and quilt according to your favorite method. Bind and label your quilt.

Quilt assembly

REFLECTIONS, 46½" x 54½", designed, pieced, and quilted by the author

This quilt demonstrates one of the many variations possible with the Hill & Valley blocks. This quilt uses 16 V4 blocks with a slight variation. In order to get a more curved effect, I reduced the log width by half. In addition, I changed the configuration by having the wider logs extend to the sides. The altered V4 block, with piecing directions, is shown in Figure 1. I also modified the V4-V2 block by using half-inch logs. The modified V4-V2 blocks, with piecing directions, is shown in Figure 2, see below. (You need 16 altered V4 blocks, 68 modified V4-V2 blocks in six colorways, and 36 plain blocks.) Fabrics were limited to four: tan, brown, ivory and purple. Make the blocks following the piecing order given on pages 70–73.

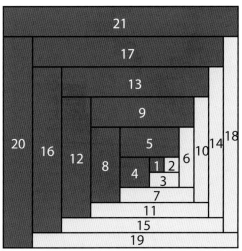

Figure 1. Altered V4 block

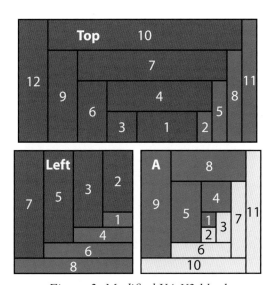

Figure 2. Modified V4-V2 block

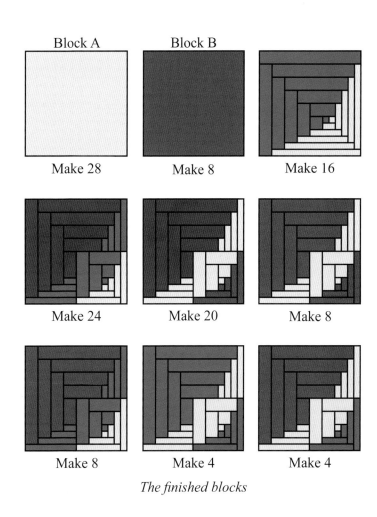

Block A — Make 28
Block B — Make 8
Make 16
Make 24
Make 20
Make 8
Make 8
Make 4
Make 4

The finished blocks

Materials

Purple: 1⅛ yards	Ivory: 1½ yards
Brown: 1⅛ yards	Tan: 1½ yards

Cutting Directions

All measurements are in inches.

Blocks A and B				
Section	**Fabric**	**Width**	**Length**	**Cut**
Block A	Ivory	4½	4½	28
Block B	Tan	4½	4½	8

Cutting Directions

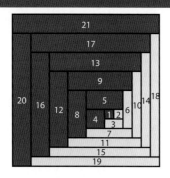

Block C

All measurements are in inches.

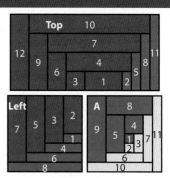

Block D

All measurements are in inches.

Block C: AV4				
Fabric	Piece	Width	Length	Cut
Purple	1	¾	¾	16
Purple	4	1	1	16
Purple	5	1	1½	16
Purple	8	1	1¾	16
Purple	9	1	2¼	16
Purple	12	1	2½	16
Purple	13	1	3	16
Purple	16	1	3¼	16
Purple	17	1	3¾	16
Purple	20	1	4	16
Purple	21	1	4½	16
Ivory	2	¾	¾	16
Ivory	3	¾	1	16
Ivory	6	¾	1½	16
Ivory	7	¾	1¾	16
Ivory	10	¾	2¼	16
Ivory	11	¾	2½	16
Ivory	14	¾	3	16
Ivory	15	¾	3¼	16
Ivory	18	¾	3¾	16
Ivory	19	¾	4	16
Purple	Border 1	1	40	5
Brown	Border 2	1½	40	5
Tan	Border 3	2	40	5
Tan	Binding	2½	40	5

Modified Block D: V4-V2					
Section	Fabric	Piece	Width	Length	Cut
Top	Purple	2	¾	1	24
	Purple	5	¾	1½	24
	Purple	8	¾	2	24
	Purple	11	¾	2½	24
	Brown	1	1	1½	24
	Brown	3	1	1	24
	Brown	4	1	2¼	24
	Brown	6	1	1½	24
	Brown	7	1	3	24
	Brown	9	1	2	24
	Brown	10	1	3¾	24
	Brown	12	1	2½	24
Left	Purple	1	¾	1	24
	Purple	4	¾	1½	24
	Purple	6	¾	2	24
	Purple	8	¾	2½	24
	Brown	2	1	1½	24
	Brown	3	1	1¾	24
	Brown	5	1	2	24
	Brown	7	1	2¼	24
A	Purple	1	¾	¾	24
	Purple	4	1	1	24
	Purple	5	1	1½	24
	Purple	8	1	1¾	24
	Purple	9	1	2¼	24
	Ivory	2	¾	¾	24
	Ivory	3	¾	1	24
	Ivory	6	¾	1½	24
	Ivory	7	¾	1¾	24
	Ivory	10	¾	2¼	24
	Ivory	11	¾	2½	24

Cutting Directions

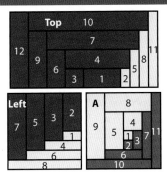

Block E

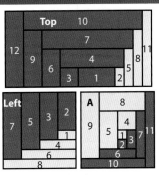

Block F

All measurements are in inches.

Modified Block E: V4-V2					
Section	Fabric	Piece	Width	Length	Cut
Top	Ivory	2	¾	1	20
	Ivory	5	¾	1½	20
	Ivory	8	¾	2	20
	Ivory	11	¾	2½	20
	Brown	1	1	1½	20
	Brown	3	1	1	20
	Brown	4	1	2¼	20
	Brown	6	1	1½	20
	Brown	7	1	3	20
	Brown	9	1	2	20
	Brown	10	1	3¾	20
	Brown	12	1	2½	20
Left	Ivory	1	¾	1	20
	Ivory	4	¾	1½	20
	Ivory	6	¾	2	20
	Ivory	8	¾	2½	20
	Brown	2	1	1½	20
	Brown	3	1	1¾	20
	Brown	5	1	2	20
	Brown	7	1	2¼	20
A	Ivory	1	¾	¾	20
	Ivory	4	1	1	20
	Ivory	5	1	1½	20
	Ivory	8	1	1¾	20
	Ivory	9	1	2¼	20
	Tan	2	¾	¾	20
	Tan	3	¾	1	20
	Tan	6	¾	1½	20
	Tan	7	¾	1¾	20
	Tan	10	¾	2¼	20
	Tan	11	¾	2½	20

All measurements are in inches.

Modified Block F : V4-V2					
Section	Fabric	Piece	Width	Length	Cut
Top	Ivory	2	¾	1	8
	Ivory	5	¾	1½	8
	Ivory	8	¾	2	8
	Ivory	11	¾	2½	8
	Tan	1	1	1½	8
	Tan	3	1	1	8
	Tan	4	1	2¼	8
	Tan	6	1	1½	8
	Tan	7	1	3	8
	Tan	9	1	2	8
	Tan	10	1	3¾	8
	Tan	12	1	2½	8
Left	Ivory	1	¾	1	8
	Ivory	4	¾	1½	8
	Ivory	6	¾	2	8
	Ivory	8	¾	2½	8
	Tan	2	1	1½	8
	Tan	3	1	1¾	8
	Tan	5	1	2	8
	Tan	7	1	2¼	8
A	Ivory	1	¾	¾	8
	Ivory	4	1	1	8
	Ivory	5	1	1½	8
	Ivory	8	1	1¾	8
	Ivory	9	1	2¼	8
	Tan	2	¾	¾	8
	Tan	3	¾	1	8
	Tan	6	¾	1½	8
	Tan	7	¾	1¾	8
	Tan	10	¾	2¼	8
	Tan	11	¾	2½	8

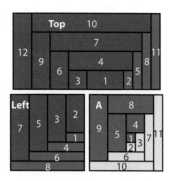

Block G

All measurements are in inches.

Modified Block G : V4-V2					
Section	Fabric	Piece	Width	Length	Cut
Top	Purple	2	¾	1	8
	Purple	5	¾	1½	8
	Purple	8	¾	2	8
	Purple	11	¾	2½	8
	Tan	1	1	1½	8
	Tan	3	1	1	8
	Tan	4	1	2¼	8
	Tan	6	1	1½	8
	Tan	7	1	3	8
	Tan	9	1	2	8
	Tan	10	1	3¾	8
	Tan	12	1	2½	8
Left	Purple	1	¾	1	8
	Purple	4	¾	1½	8
	Purple	6	¾	2	8
	Purple	8	¾	2½	8
	Tan	2	1	1½	8
	Tan	3	1	1¾	8
	Tan	5	1	2	8
	Tan	7	1	2¼	8
A	Purple	1	¾	¾	8
	Purple	4	1	1	8
	Purple	5	1	1½	8
	Purple	8	1	1¾	8
	Purple	9	1	2¼	8
	Ivory	2	¾	¾	8
	Ivory	3	¾	1	8
	Ivory	6	¾	1½	8
	Ivory	7	¾	1¾	8
	Ivory	10	¾	2¼	8
	Ivory	11	¾	2½	8

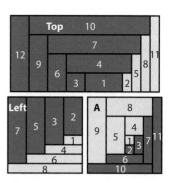

Block H

All measurements are in inches.

Modified Block H : V4-V2					
Section	Fabric	Piece	Width	Length	Cut
Top	Ivory	2	¾	1	4
	Ivory	5	¾	1½	4
	Ivory	8	¾	2	4
	Ivory	11	¾	2½	4
	Purple	1	1	1½	4
	Purple	3	1	1	4
	Purple	4	1	2¼	4
	Purple	6	1	1½	4
	Purple	7	1	3	4
	Purple	9	1	2	4
	Purple	10	1	3¾	4
	Purple	12	1	2½	4
Left	Ivory	1	¾	1	4
	Ivory	4	¾	1½	4
	Ivory	6	¾	2	4
	Ivory	8	¾	2½	4
	Purple	2	1	1½	4
	Purple	3	1	1¾	4
	Purple	5	1	2	4
	Purple	7	1	2¼	4
A	Ivory	1	¾	¾	4
	Ivory	4	1	1	4
	Ivory	5	1	1½	4
	Ivory	8	1	1¾	4
	Ivory	9	1	2¼	4
	Purple	2	¾	¾	4
	Purple	3	¾	1	4
	Purple	6	¾	1½	4
	Purple	7	¾	1¾	4
	Purple	10	¾	2¼	4
	Purple	11	¾	2½	4

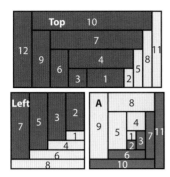

Block I

All measurements are in inches.

Section	Fabric	Piece	Width	Length	Cut
Top	Ivory	2	¾	1	4
	Ivory	5	¾	1½	4
	Ivory	8	¾	2	4
	Ivory	11	¾	2½	4
	Tan	1	1	1½	4
	Tan	3	1	1	4
	Tan	4	1	2¼	4
	Tan	6	1	1½	4
	Tan	7	1	3	4
	Tan	9	1	2	4
	Tan	10	1	3¾	4
	Tan	12	1	2½	4
Left	Ivory	1	¾	1	4
	Ivory	4	¾	1½	4
	Ivory	6	¾	2	4
	Ivory	8	¾	2½	4
	Tan	2	1	1½	4
	Tan	3	1	1¾	4
	Tan	5	1	2	4
	Tan	7	1	2¼	4
A	Ivory	1	¾	¾	4
	Ivory	4	1	1	4
	Ivory	5	1	1½	4
	Ivory	8	1	1¾	4
	Ivory	9	1	2¼	4
	Purple	2	¾	¾	4
	Purple	3	¾	1	4
	Purple	6	¾	1½	4
	Purple	7	¾	1¾	4
	Purple	10	¾	2¼	4
	Purple	11	¾	2½	4

*Table title: **Modified Block I : V4-V2***

Quilt Construction

Lay out the blocks according to the quilt assembly diagram (page 75). The blocks are turned once, twice, or three times clockwise to construct the quilt.

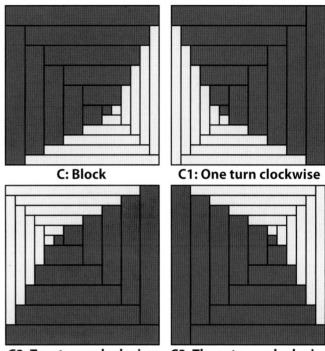

C: Block **C1: One turn clockwise**

C2: Two turns clockwise **C3: Three turns clockwise**

Block orientation

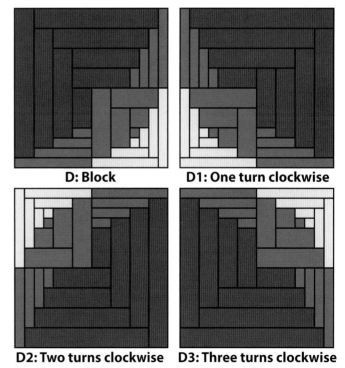

D: Block **D1: One turn clockwise**

D2: Two turns clockwise **D3: Three turns clockwise**

Block orientation

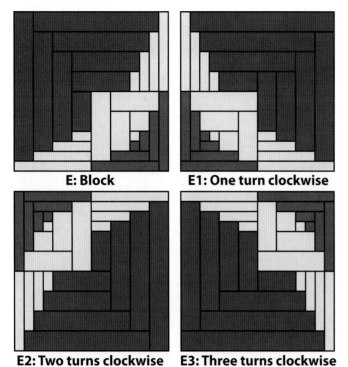

E: Block   **E1: One turn clockwise**

E2: Two turns clockwise   **E3: Three turns clockwise**

Block orientation

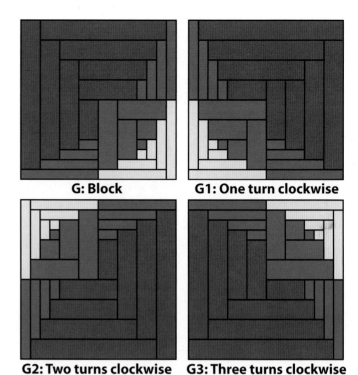

G: Block   **G1: One turn clockwise**

G2: Two turns clockwise   **G3: Three turns clockwise**

Block orientation

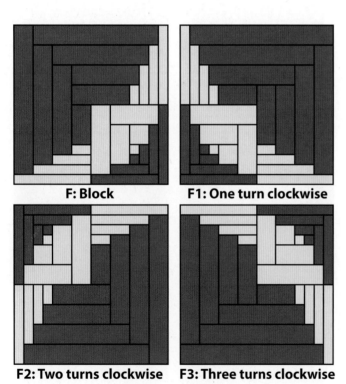

F: Block   **F1: One turn clockwise**

F2: Two turns clockwise   **F3: Three turns clockwise**

Block orientation

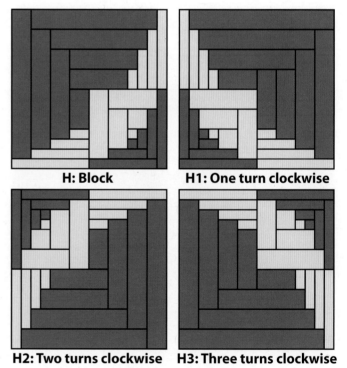

H: Block   **H1: One turn clockwise**

H2: Two turns clockwise   **H3: Three turns clockwise**

Block orientation

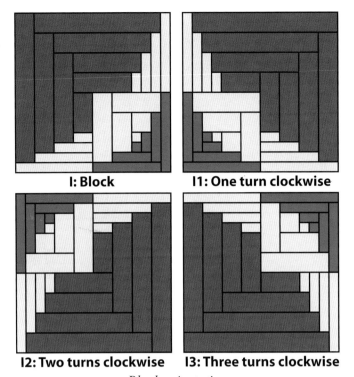

I: Block **I1: One turn clockwise**

I2: Two turns clockwise **I3: Three turns clockwise**

Block orientation

Cut 2 border strips 1" x 48½" from the purple. Sew to the sides of the quilt. Cut 2 border strips 1½" x 41½" from the purple.

Sew to the top and bottom of the quilt.

Cut 2 border strips 1½" x 49½" from the brown and sew to the sides of the quilt.

Cut 2 border strips 1½" x 43½" from the brown and sew to the top and bottom of the quilt.

Cut 2 border strips 2" x 51½" from the tan and sew to the sides of the quilt.

Cut 2 border strips 2" x 46½" from the tan and sew to the top and bottom of the quilt.

Layer and quilt according to your favorite method. Bind and label your quilt.

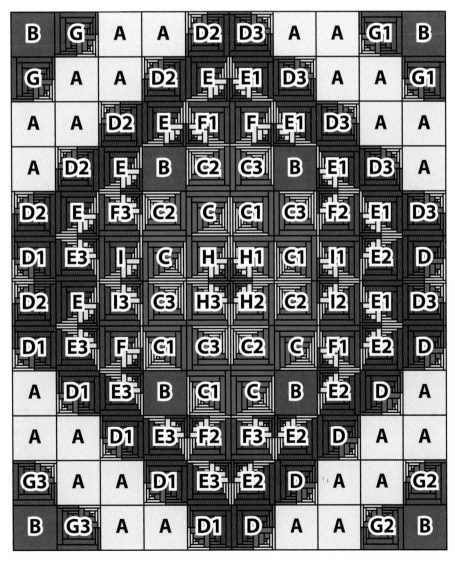

Variations on a Theme

Eleven Hill & Valley Log Cabin blocks are sufficient to generate a seemingly infinite number of quilts. You can use any of the blocks in any of the quilt projects presented here and get a strikingly different and beautiful quilt.

For example, the SUNBURST quilt (page 32) layout looks completely different when some of the blocks are replaced with Valley8-Valley4-Hill2 blocks.

Figure 1. SUNBURST layout and variation

With different fabrics and yet another layout, you get an entirely new look.

Figure 2. Original design featuring the V8-V4 block

You could work with the basic Log Cabin set forever and never exhaust the possibilities, but there is another world (actually several) beyond that we can explore.

Out of the Valley to the Mountain

If you turn the Valley8 (V8) block twice clockwise, you get a Hill effect, which we call the Hill8 (H8) block.

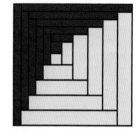

Figure 3. The Hill8 (H8) block.

In the lower right, you can carve out a 4" square basically along the seam lines. This breaks the block into three sections, the Top, Left, and 4" square.

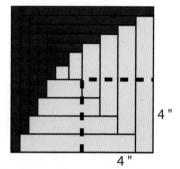

Figure 4. Carving out a 4" section

The 4" square can be used for a V4 block, a H4 block, a V4-V2 block, a V4-H2 block, a H4-V2 block, or a H4-H2 block. This gives us a completely new set of blocks.

Here is another variation of the SUNBURST quilt featuring the H8-H4 block.

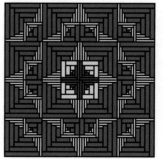 

Figure 5. SUNBURST variation

Bigger Isn't Better, Just Bigger

Suppose you wanted a queen- or king-size quilt. One approach is to simply make more of the 8" blocks and repeat the design around the outside. An alternative approach is to use bigger blocks.

It turns out that everything we did to the 8" block works equally well on a 12" Curved Log Cabin block. Cut a 6" square (from either corner) and replace it with a 6" Curved Log Cabin block or a 6" block with a 3" block inserted in its corner.

The center section of the Valley configuration of a 12" Curved Log Cabin block (Valley configuration) is two ¾" (finished) squares attached to a ¾" x 1½" strip. The rest of the logs are ½" (finished) and 1" (finished) strips.

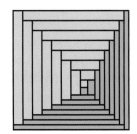

Figure 6. 12" Curved Log Cabin block

On the bottom right corner you can carve out a 6" square, resulting in 3 sections.

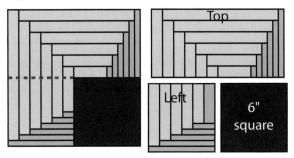

Figure 7. 12" Curved Log Cabin block in sections

The top and left sections are log-like and pieced accordingly. Replace the 6" square with a 6" Curved Log Cabin block (figure 9) or a 6" block with a 3" insert (figure 10).

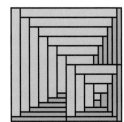

Figure 8. V12 block with V6 insert

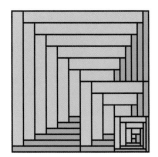

Figure 9. V12 block with V6-V3 insert

You can use the 6" block in either the Valley or Hill configuration. Similarly, the 3" insert can be used in either configuration. This process generates the same set of blocks as we had for the 8" blocks.

Too much of a good thing is, of course, even better. So you can do the same thing with the opposite corner—the Hill part. Look at the construction of the 12" block and note that you can carve a 6" square out of the upper right corner, giving three sections (just as for the 8").

You can insert a 6" block in either configuration and further, insert a 3" block in either corner of that block.

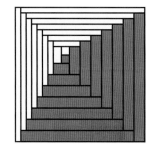

Curved 12" Hill log block

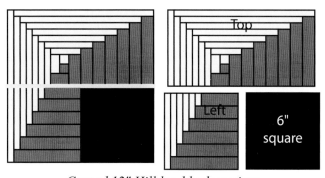

Curved 12" Hill log block sections

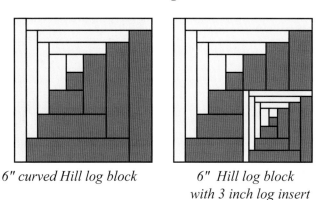

6" curved Hill log block   *6" Hill log block with 3 inch log insert*

You can make all the quilts in this book using 12" blocks.

Straight "Ain't" Curvy but It's Cool

Everything that applies to the Curved Log Cabin block applies equally well to the traditional (straight) Log Cabin block. You can carve a 6" square from the corner of a 12" block, resulting in three sections—just as for the curved block.

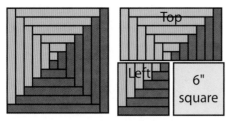

Figure 10. The 12" straight Log Cabin block and its sections

Replace the 6" square with a 6" straight Log Cabin block or any of the curved variations.

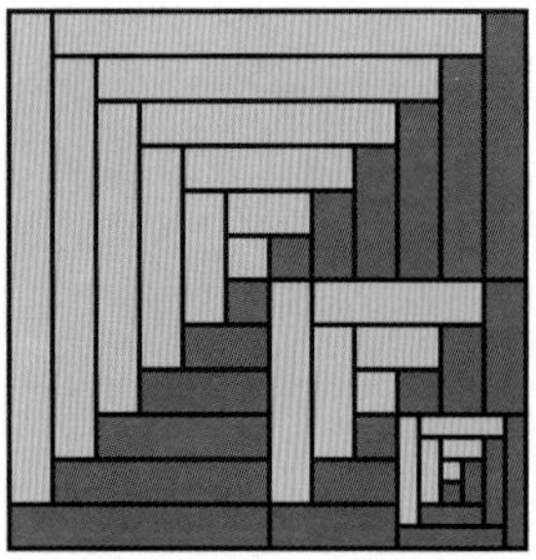

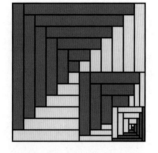

Figure 11. Straight 12" block with straight 6" and 3" inserts

You can also use any of the blocks previously developed—V6, H6, V6-V3, V6-H3, or H6-H3. You can mix and match the straight with the curved.

Figure 12. 12" straight block with V6-V3 block insert

Here again is SUNBURST with yet another variation.

Figure 13. SUNBURST with straight 12" blocks with curved V6-V3 block insert

The process can be applied to the full spectrum of 8" and 12" Log Cabin blocks.

Start with a block, straight or curved. From either the top left corner or the bottom right corner, carve out a square half the size of the original block. Replace the square with a straight or curved (Valley or Hill) block, or a straight or curved block with a straight or curved (Valley or Hill) smaller insert. Each of the blocks generated will make an endless number of quilts.

The End of the Road—Maybe

The basic "block in a block in a block" process generates a large number of blocks. We have:

8" curved log (Valley) with a 4" Valley insert
8" curved log (Valley) with a 4" Hill insert
8" curved log (Valley) with a 4" Valley insert with a 2" Valley insert
8" curved log (Valley) with a 4" Valley insert with a 2" Hill insert
8" curved log (Valley) with a 4" Hill insert with a 2" Valley insert
8" curved log (Valley) with a 4" Hill insert with a 2" Hill insert
8" curved log (Hill) with a 4" Valley insert
8" curved log (Hill) with a 4" Hill insert
8" curved log (Hill) with a 4" Valley insert with a 2" Valley insert
8" curved log (Hill) with a 4" Valley insert with a 2" Hill insert
8" curved log (Hill) with a 4" Hill insert with a 2" Valley insert
8" curved log (Hill) with a 4" Hill insert with a 2" Hill insert
1 – 12 above using 12, 6 and 3 in place of the 8, 4, and 2
1 – 8 above using the 8" straight block in place of the curved
1 – 8 above using the 12" straight block in place of the curved
8 (or 12)" straight with a 4 (or 6)" straight insert
8 (or 12)" straight with a 4 (or 6)" and a 2 (or 3)" insert
Mix and match: any straight or curved with any straight or curved (Hill or Valley) insert or any straight or curved with any straight or curved (Hill or Valley) insert with any straight or curved (Hill or Valley) smaller insert.

You would think that this would be enough but we can even extend the process to non-square Log Cabin blocks.

If you look at the construction of the 45-degree 12" (or 8") Log Cabin block, straight or curved, you will see that you can carve a 45-degree piece (along seam lines) from the corner (and a 45-degree piece from this piece as well), again resulting in three sections similar to the what we have for the straight or curved blocks.

You can replace the cut-out piece with a 45-degree log block (Valley, Hill. or straight) or put a block in a block as we did for the straight (or curved) block. This gives another set of blocks, two of which are shown in figures 14 and 15.

Figure 14
45-degree block
with Hill insert

Figure 15
45-degree block with Valley
insert within the Valley insert

Meet Bob DeCarli

Photo by Kathleen DeCarli

Bob's first life was as a math professor at a Catholic girls college in Buffalo, New York. He moved on to function as an engineer at Lockheed Martin in Valley Forge, Pennsylvania, all the while continuing to teach math at local colleges. In 1992 his wife, Kathleen, asked for help in making a quilt for their daughter's wedding. She showed him how to make a Four-Patch and he was hooked.

As a mathematician, the seemingly endless number of possible patterns fascinated him. He has designed blocks and quilts since 1993, receiving a ribbon at the Vermont Quilt Festival and a blue ribbon at the Pennsylvania Quilt Extravaganza for BUTTERFLY (designed in EQ5).

He discovered Electric Quilt software in 2005 and has since designed more than 1,000 quilts and blocks, including block and quilt settings for his wife's appliqué projects. His primary interest, besides teaching, is designing various-sized, interlocking Log Cabin blocks and converting weaving patterns into quilts. In each area, the number of possibilities is seemingly endless, but he pursues them one at a time.

More AQS Books

This is only a small selection of the books available from the American Quilter's Society. AQS books are known worldwide for timely topics, clear writing, beautiful color photos, and accurate illustrations and patterns. The following books are available from your local bookseller, quilt shop, or public library.

#8768 $26.95

#8147 $28.95

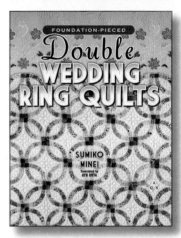

#8765 $19.95

#8662 $26.95

#8761 $21.95

#8767 $21.95

#8664 $19.95

#8663 $24.95

#8346 $26.95